270   280   290   300   310   320   330

BAFFINS BAY

ARCTICK LAND

D... STRAITS

NEW NORTH WALES

NEW SOUTH WALES

HUDSONS BAY

Hudsons Straits

TERRA LABRADOR

NEW BRITAIN

NEW FOUND LAND

The Main Bank

False Bank

James

LAKE SUPERIOR

LAKE HURON

ILINOIS

LAKE ERIE

NEW FRANCE

PENN...

MAR... VIRG...

CARO...

50

40

SEA OF THE ENGLISH EMPIRE

Bermudos als Summer Island

30

THE GOLF or BAY OF MEXICO

FLORIDA

BAHAMA ISLANDS

ANTILLES Is   WEST INDIAN

20

SEA

CARIBY ISLANDS

YUCATAN

GOLF...

10

280   290   300   310   320

· VOICES · *from* COLONIAL AMERICA

RHODE ISLAND

1636 — 1776

JESSE McDERMOTT

WITH

BRENDAN McCONVILLE, PH.D., CONSULTANT

NATIONAL GEOGRAPHIC

WASHINGTON, D.C.

Text copyright © 2006 National Geographic Society
Published by the National Geographic Society.
All rights reserved. Reproduction of the whole or any part of the contents without written permission from the National Geographic Society is strictly prohibited. For information about special discounts for bulk purchases, please contact National Geographic Books Special Sales: ngspecsales@ngs.org

John M. Fahey, Jr., *President and Chief Executive Officer*
Gilbert M. Grosvenor, *Chairman of the Board*
Nina D. Hoffman, *Executive Vice President, President Book Publishing Group*

STAFF FOR THIS BOOK

Nancy Laties Feresten, *Vice President, Editor-in-Chief of Children's Books*
Suzanne Patrick Fonda, *Project Editor*
Robert D. Johnston, Ph.D., *Associate Professor and Director, Teaching of History Program University of Illinois at Chicago, Series Editor*
Bea Jackson, *Director of Illustration and Design, Children's Books*
Jean Cantu, *Illustrations Specialist*
Carl Mehler, *Director of Maps*
Justin Morrill, *The M Factory, Inc., Map Research, Design, and Production*
Rebecca Baines, *Editorial Assistant*
Rebecca Hinds, *Managing Editor*
Connie Binder, *Indexer*
R. Gary Colbert, *Production Director*
Lewis R. Bassford, *Production Manager*
Vincent P. Ryan and Maryclare Tracy, *Manufacturing Managers*

Voices from Colonial Delaware was prepared by
CREATIVE MEDIA APPLICATIONS, INC.

Jesse McDermott, *Writer*
Fabia Wargin Design, Inc., *Design and Production*
Susan Madoff, *Editor*
Laurie Lieb, *Copyeditor*
Jennifer Bright, *Image Researcher*

Body text is set in Deepdene, sidebars are Caslon 337 Oldstyle, and display text is Cochin Archaic Bold.

LIBRARY OF CONGRESS CATALOGING-IN-PUBLICATION DATA
McDermott, Jesse.
  Voices from Colonial America. Rhode Island, 1636–1776 / by Jesse McDermott.
    p. cm. — (Voices from Colonial America)
  Includes bibliographical references and index.
  ISBN-10: 0-7922-6410-X (Hardcover)
  ISBN-13: 978-0-7922-6410-1 (Hardcover)
  ISBN-10: 0-7922-6868-7 (Library)
  ISBN-13: 978-0-7922-6868-0 (Library)
  1. Rhode Island—History—Colonial period, ca. 1600–1775 —Juvenile literature. I. National Geographic Society (U.S.) II. Title. III. Title: Rhode Island, 1636–1776.
  F82.M33 2006
  974.5'02—dc22
                                        2006018139

Printed in Belgium

CONTENTS

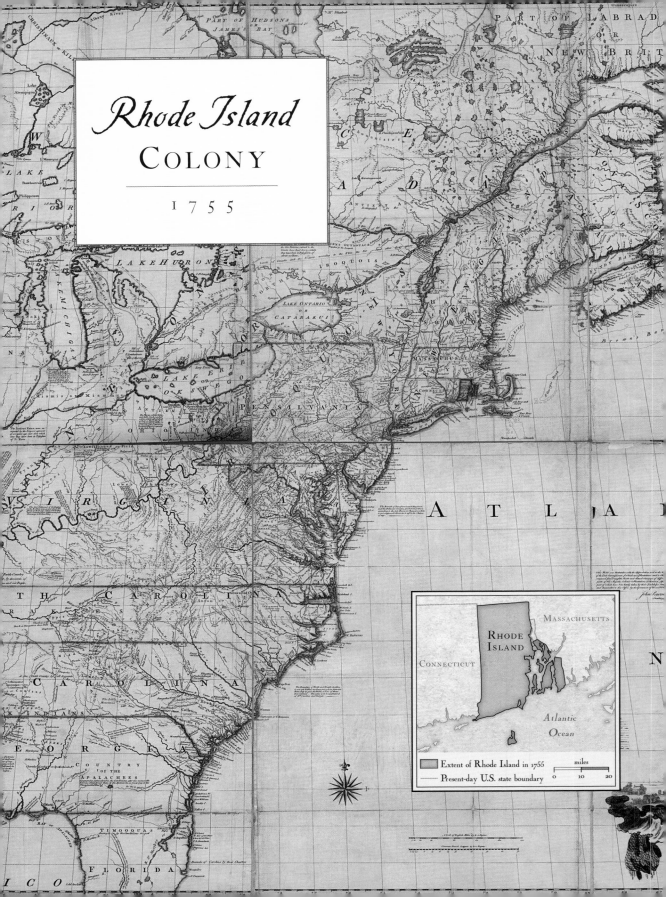

Rhode Island
COLONY

1755

Extent of Rhode Island in 1755

Present-day U.S. state boundary

MASSACHUSETTS

RHODE ISLAND

CONNECTICUT

Atlantic Ocean

miles

0   10   20

INTRODUCTION

by

Brendan McConville, Ph.D.

The Quaker Meetinghouse at Newport, Rhode Island

Take a look at Rhode Island on a map of the United States. How could such a small state come into being in such a vast continent, squeezed into a corner in southern New England? Where did it come from and how did it survive as a distinctive place? And how did the values we associate with Rhode Island—tolerance, religious variety, and Yankee ingenuity—come to be the hallmarks of the colony and state?

OPPOSITE: This historical map, created by John Mitchell in 1755, has been colorized to emphasize the boundaries of the Rhode Island colony. The inset map shows the state's present-day boundaries for comparison.

To answer these questions we need to think back to the beginning of the Puritan settlements in New England in the 1620s and 1630s. And we need to let the early mansions of Providence, the ancient stone walls separating the fields of Tiverton and Little Compton, and the churches and synagogues in coastal Newport speak to us now. When we do, we understand how Rhode Island came to be and the enduring importance of the state's colonial history to the society we live in now.

From its very beginning, Rhode Island was distinctive. The exiles from the infant settlements in Massachusetts and Connecticut and unwanted Protestants from across England and Europe fled or were forced to Rhode Island because of their spiritual and political beliefs. From the fragmented settlements of refugees that appeared in the 1630s, a new colony with unique values was created. In a world rife with religious wars and spiritual persecution, these exiles bravely proclaimed freedom of worship for Protestants. As the settlers in colonies around them seized the lands of Native Americans by fraud and war, the people of Rhode Island purchased the grounds for their farmsteads and fields, only entering wars between Native Americans and other colonists in self-defense.

By the 18th century, the colony began to prosper as its people turned to the Atlantic to trade and fish. The inlets of Narragansett Bay became ports connected to the broader world, and Rhode Island ships created important threads tying that world together, for better and worse. Rum, agricultural goods, timber, and African slaves were moved around the Atlantic by merchants with their homes along Narragansett Bay. Traders sailing from Newport and Providence linked North America, Europe, Africa, and the Caribbean.

This volume of *Voices from Colonial America* acts as the link between these colonial Rhode Islanders and you, the reader. You will discover that the lessons of that time are as relevant today as they were 300 years ago.

A copy of the 1663 Royal Charter of Rhode Island is illustrated with a picture of King Charles II.

CHAPTER ONE

The Settlement at Providence

THE REVEREND ROGER WILLIAMS *arrives in Massachusetts Bay but is soon banished for his unpopular religious beliefs. He searches for a place to settle where he can freely worship and preach religious tolerance.*

 hode Island's story begins with a man named Roger Williams. Williams was a minister who was forced to leave Massachusetts because of his unpopular religious views. In spite of his difficulties, Williams went on to found Providence, the first settlement in what would become known as Rhode Island.

OPPOSITE: Roger Williams, the founder of Rhode Island, in an engraving by Frederick W. Halpern.

THE FIRST EUROPEAN

In the 1520s, the east coast of America had still not been fully explored. European rulers were sending expeditions to America for many reasons. The explorers hoped that by sailing west, they could reach India and China faster than they could by using the known land and sea routes. America had once been thought to be these eastern lands; now, the explorers were looking for a route around America. The Spanish had already found gold in South America, so the explorers were also looking for any treasure they could bring back.

Giovanni da Verrazano was the first to chart the coastline that would eventually include the English colony of Rhode Island.

In 1524, King Francis I of France decided to send Giovanni da Verrazano on just such an expedition. Verrazano sailed from France to America, arriving off the shores of what are now the Carolinas. From there, he sailed north, visiting what became known as Narragansett Bay and charting the coastline as far as Maine. After stopping in present-day New York Harbor, he followed the coast until, as he later wrote, *"we discovered an Island in the form of a triangle, . . . about the bigness of the Island of Rhodes [in Greece]. It was full of hills covered with trees, well peopled, for we saw fires all along the coast."*

Verrazano stayed in the harbor for two weeks while he waited for good weather to continue his voyage. During that time, he and his crew traded with the Wampanoag Indians who lived in the area, and he wrote very kindly about them, describing how they lived, some of their customs, and their generous nature. After Verrazano's departure, it would take more than 100 years before the tiny region we now call Rhode Island would again be of interest to a European.

WILLIAMS ARRIVES IN AMERICA

On February 9, 1631, the ship *Lyon* dropped anchor outside of Boston, the capital of Massachusetts Bay Colony. Waiting aboard the *Lyon* was Roger Williams, a young Protestant minister, and his wife, Mary. Williams was a Puritan who, throughout his life, had stood up for what he believed in, even if it meant trouble or hardship for him. Later in his life, Williams recalled that *"[God] knows what gains and preferments I have refused in universities, city, county and court in Old England . . . to keep my soul undefiled in this point and not to act with a doubting conscience."*

Protestant—a person who follows a Christian faith established in the 16th century in protest against certain Catholic policies

Puritan—a Protestant whose faith was based on the Bible rather than the teachings of church leaders

In the two years before his journey, Williams had been the chaplain to a wealthy family in Essex, England. During this time, Williams became convinced that people should be free to pursue whatever religion they desired and that religion and government should be separate. This belief led Williams to leave England.

chaplain—a member of the clergy who is connected with a family, court, the military, or other institution

Puritans seeking a place where they can worship in peace wait on the shore to board ships that will take them to the New World. Men, women, and small children, some kneeling in prayer, look toward an oncoming crowd who, they hope, will not delay their departure.

PURITANS AND SEPARATISTS

In the 1530s, England had severed relations with the Roman Catholic Church, and King Henry VIII took the place of the pope as the head of a new church. The new official religion, called the Church of England, still followed many Catholic traditions, and some people were unhappy with this. They were called Puritans. Even though they were still part of the Church of England, they wanted to reform it.

Puritans believed in a simple, pure church in which people could have a personal relationship with God without the need for priests, bishops, and archbishops. Puritans thought that they could develop this relationship by reading the Bible, praying, and listening to sermons by passionate pastors. Puritans believed in hard work and discipline, and they avoided games and other entertainment. A Puritan once explained, *"God sent you unto this world as unto [into] a Workhouse, not a Playhouse."* A group of Puritans now known as Pilgrims settled Plymouth Colony, and other Puritans settled Massachusetts Bay Colony.

When Roger Williams arrived in Massachusetts Bay Colony in 1631, he found life there more like Old England than he had expected. Although technically a separation existed between the church and the government, there was no real freedom of religious thought and speech. The laws were based on the Bible, so ministers could punish people for going against biblical teachings.

Upon Williams's arrival in Boston, the governor of Massachusetts Bay Colony, John Winthrop, immediately asked him to be a teacher at the First Church in Boston. Winthrop welcomed Williams because he expected that Williams would follow the church's rules. Williams's religious ideas, however, were more like those of the Separatists. The church in Boston still used the Church of England's prayer book, and many of the people retained an attachment to the church they had left behind. When Williams learned of these things, he refused to take the post. His conscience would not allow him to work with what he called an "unseparated" people.

Separatist—a Puritan who wanted to break away completely from the Church of England

The church in Salem where Roger Williams hoped to preach. Church leaders feared his Separatist ideas.

Williams stopped briefly in the town of Salem, which was part of Massachusetts Bay Colony, but the church leaders in Boston had warned the Salem church not to hire Williams as a minister. Williams moved on to Plymouth Colony, where he found a "separated" church. He stayed there as an assistant to the minister for almost two years. Of his time in Plymouth, Williams wrote, *"I spake on the Lord's days and week days and wrought hard at the hoe for my bread."* Governor Bradford of Plymouth described Williams and his reasons for leaving Plymouth in his history of the colony:

> Mr. Roger Williams (a man godly and zealous, . . .) came hither
> . . . and exercised his gifts . . . , and after some time was admitted
> a member of ye church . . . . He this year (1633) began to fall
> into some strange opinions . . . which caused some controversie
> between ye church and him, and in ye ende some discontente on his
> part, [and because of this] he left them some thing abruptly.

Williams brought his "strange opinions" back to Salem, where the church by this time was "separated." Some of his opinions had to do with minor points of church etiquette. For example, he taught that women should wear veils over their faces in church. Other ideas, however, were a direct result of his strong belief that church and state must be separate for there to be true freedom of religious thought and speech. In particular, Williams taught that the magistrates should not have the power to punish people for offenses against God if there was no public harm involved.

In December 1633, Williams wrote an essay claiming that the charter given to Massachusetts Bay Colony was illegal because the lands had been inhabited by Native Americans before the English. According to Governor Winthrop of Massachusetts Bay, Williams *"disputed [the Bay*

etiquette—rules governing socially acceptable behavior

magistrate—a public official authorized to decide questions brought before a court of justice

charter—a written document that grants a colony certain rights and privileges, including the right to exist

Colony's] right to the lands they possessed here, and concluded that, claiming by the King's grant, they could have no title . . . except [if] they compounded [made a business deal] with the natives."

The King's grant declared that the colony had the right to use the land, and it provided a legal foundation for the colony's government. Williams's essay upset the magistrates, because it seemed to call the King a liar and a thief. For Williams to suggest that the Indians were the only ones who could give the colonists the right to live on and use the land was shocking.

Between 1633 and 1635, Williams repeatedly fought with the colony's officials. Finally, the colony could no longer tolerate Williams and his disruptive opinions. In October 1635, the magistrates banished him from Massachusetts Bay. The official decree stated:

decree——an authoritative order having the force of law

> Whereas Mr. Roger Williams, one of the elders of the church at Salem, hath broached and divulged dyvers [diverse] newe and dangerous opinions, against the authority of magistrates, as also writ lres [letters] of defamacon [defamation], both of magistrates & churches here . . . it is therefore ordered that the same Mr. Williams shall dpte [depart] out of this jurisdiccon [jurisdiction] within six weeks . . . not to return any more without written license from the Court.

The sentence was not immediately carried out, however, because it was winter, and Williams had health problems.

The magistrates allowed him to stay in the colony until spring, on the condition that he would stop teaching his "newe and dangerous" ideas. Williams, however, continued to invite people to his house and preach to them. When the colony officials found out, they decided to put Williams on the next ship bound for England, where he would face more severe punishment for his opinions. Williams refused to travel to Boston to board the ship. When Bay Colony officials came to escort him to Boston, they discovered that Williams, warned of their coming, had already left Salem. His family joined him later.

Roger Williams struggles through the snowy wilderness as he leaves Massachusetts Bay and makes his way toward what will become Rhode Island.

Three or four other men, who felt oppressed in Massachusetts or, like him, had been banished, accompanied Williams on his departure from the Bay Colony. During the winter of 1636, Williams journeyed through the rugged, snowy wilderness, searching for a place to live. He would later write, *"I was unmercifully driven from my chamber to a winter's flight, exposed to the miseries, poverties, necessities, wants, debts, hardships, of sea and land, in a banished condition. For one fourteen weeks, in a bitter winter season, I was sorely tossed and knew not what bread or bed did mean."* Eventually, a messenger from Governor Winthrop found Williams and delivered some friendly advice about where Williams might find refuge. Although they disagreed about politics, Winthrop and Williams respected each other and maintained a friendship by letter for many years. Williams later recalled this time in his life:

> *Mr. Winthrop, privately wrote to me to steer my course to Narraganset Bay and Indians, [informing me of] the freeness of the place from any English claims or patents. I took his prudent notion as a hint and voice from God, and, waving all other thoughts and motions, I steered my course from Salem (though in winter snow, which I feel yet) unto these parts, wherein I may say . . . I have seen the face of God.*

At first, Williams tried to settle at a place called Seekonk, on the northeast side of the Seekonk River, then part of Plymouth Colony's lands. Williams and his group immediately began building shelter and clearing land to plant crops. Soon, however, Williams received a letter from Governor Edward Winslow of Plymouth telling him to move on. *"Since I was fallen into the edge of their bounds, and they were loath to displease [Massachusetts] Bay, to remove but to the other side of the water and there, he said, I had the country free before me and might be as free as themselves."*

Williams packed up his little group of settlers and traveled south by canoe into Narragansett Bay. They turned north around the tip of present-day East Providence and sailed until they came to a spring at the head of the bay, where two rivers met. Here Williams and company set up a small settlement. Williams named the area Providence, because he believed that God's care and guardianship had brought his group to this new home. ❈

CHAPTER TWO

Relations with Native Americans

Native Americans *compete for power, as the Pequot wage war on the English and Williams negotiates for peace.*

here were three major Native American tribes living in New England when the English settled Plymouth Colony and Massachusetts Bay Colony in the 1620s and 1630s—the Wampanoag of southeastern Massachusetts, the Narragansett of Rhode Island, and the Pequot, who lived in eastern Connecticut. These tribes all shared a language called Algonquian.

opposite: English colonists gather to joyously welcome Massasoit, the sachem of the Wampanoag. Massasoit helped the settlers survive by showing them how to plant corn, catch fish, and gather dry fruits for the long winter.

The Wampanoag lived near Plymouth Colony, between Narragansett Bay and Cape Cod. When Verrazano visited the region, this powerful tribe controlled the area around Narragansett Bay. By the time the Puritans arrived in 1630, the Wampanoag had lost much of their power and population because of two smallpox epidemics that had spread through the New England tribes between 1614 and 1620. The disease was probably spread by European explorers and slave traders. A Wampanoag chief, or sachem, named Massasoit, befriended the first European settlers of the region and helped them survive.

epidemic—an outbreak of contagious disease that spreads rapidly and widely

sachem—a chief of a Native American tribe, especially an Algonquian chief

The Narragansett, who lived in villages on the many small islands in Narragansett Bay, did not suffer from the smallpox epidemics as badly as the Wampanoag. The island villages were isolated from the mainland, so the disease did not spread to their homes. Since the Narragansett population remained stable, they became the dominant tribe in the area. They forced the Wampanoag to abandon the Narragansett Bay area and made them pay tribute, which was a sign of the Narragansett's superiority. The sachem Canonicus and his son Miantonomi led the Narragansett.

The Pequot were the largest tribe in Connecticut. In the 1620s, they often traded with the Dutch, who set up a

tribute—a payment in money or other valuables made by one ruler or nation to another in acknowledgment of the other's superiority or as the price of protection trading post in Windsor, near what is now Hartford, Connecticut. When the English arrived and set up a rival trading post near the Connecticut River in 1633, the Pequot split into two factions. One, led by the sachem Sassacus, wanted to continue trading with the Dutch. But his son-in-law Uncas favored trading with the English. The disputes became so bad that eventually Uncas and his supporters left the Pequot and began their own tribe, calling themselves Mohegan.

faction—a group of people forming a united, usually quarrelsome minority within a larger group

DAILY LIFE AMONG THE INDIANS

Despite their differences, the daily lives of these Algonquian tribes were very similar. People lived in wigwams located in small villages. Wigwams could be easily taken apart and moved. This was important because the New England Indians did not stay in the same place all year long. In summer, they lived near the coast, where they could catch fish and shellfish. They also planted crops like corn, beans, and squash. Shortly after the harvest, they moved farther inland to family hunting camps for the winter. During the cold winter months, they lived in permanent homes called longhouses, which could hold up to 20 families.

wigwam—a Native American dwelling commonly having an arched or conical framework overlaid with bark, hides, or mats

Everything the people needed came from the land and the sea, but they worked hard to get it. Women planted, cultivated, and harvested the crops. They also cooked the food, wove mats for the wigwams, raised the children, and cared for the home. Their labor left men plenty of time for their main jobs: hunting and fishing. Hunting provided not only food, but also animal skins for clothing and shoes (moccasins). Men also made wampum.

Wampum was beads made from the shells of a quahog, a kind of clam found in Narragansett Bay. Wampum played an extremely important part in Indian culture and had many uses. The beads could be strung together and used in decorating clothing or as jewelry. To the Europeans, wampum seemed to be Indian money, but it was much more important than that. Wampum could be given as a gift or a sign of respect. It showed social standing. The more wampum a person wore, the more important he or she was. Wampum was even used for storytelling, as a way of remembering important events. It was woven into belts to record treaties and agreements.

wampum—small cylindrical beads made from polished shells and fashioned into strings or belts

THE PEQUOT WAR

In 1634, the Pequot had been the only tribe trading with the Dutch in southeastern Connecticut for many years. They became upset when other tribes began trading fur there also. The Pequot attacked some Narragansett Indians at a Dutch trading post. The Dutch fought back, kidnapping and killing the chief sachem, Tatobem. Tatobem's son, Sassacus, became the chief sachem.

Later that year, an English trader and pirate named John Stone, who was on a voyage to capture Indian slaves, was killed as retribution for Tatobem's murder. When the English demanded the murderers, the Pequot responded, *"How could ye blame us for avenging so cruel a murder? For we distinguish not between Dutch and English and therefore we do not conceive that we wronged you. For they slew OUR KING!"* The Pequot could not see any difference between the Dutch and English, so they thought the English had caused Tatobem's death.

From the shoreline of Block Island, Indians defend themselves as John Endicott leads an attack during the Pequot War in 1663.

In 1636, another Englishman, Captain John Oldham of Massachusetts Bay, was killed by Indians while on a trading voyage to Block Island. Outraged, leaders in Boston sent an expedition under the command of John Endicott to punish the Pequot living on the island. Although most of the Indians had left before the colonists arrived, Endicott ordered the villages destroyed. In retaliation, the furious Pequot attacked the English settlement at Fort Saybrook in Connecticut. These events were the beginning of the Pequot War.

The Pequot sachem Sassacus knew that he would need help in fighting the English. He also knew that the Narragansett were the most powerful tribe in what is now Rhode Island. So, he set about trying to persuade Canonicus and the Narragansett to become allies of the Pequot. When news of this possible alliance reached Boston, the Bay Colony acted to stop it, fearing that the united tribes could wipe out the Puritan settlers.

Bay Colony officials knew that the Indians respected Roger Williams and that he might be able to prevent the deadly alliance. Williams's friendship with the chief sachems of the Wampanoag and the Narragansett had begun at Plymouth in 1631. In the next two years he spent a lot of time living with the Wampanoag, learning their language in an effort to convert them to Christianity. Williams was very good with languages, so he learned Algonquian quickly. He wrote, *"God was pleased to give me a painful Patient spirit to lodge with [the Wampanoag], in their filthy smoke holes . . .*

to gain their tongue." Both tribes thought of Williams as a good friend. In 1636, the Bay Colony wrote to Williams and asked him to help prevent the Indian alliance.

Williams set off at once. Traveling in a small canoe on rough and stormy waters, he headed to Canonicus's village, where the Pequot envoys were already trying to turn the Narragansett against the English. Williams was successful in preventing the Indian alliance. In fact, he was able to persuade the Narragansett to help Massachusetts instead.

envoy—a representative of a government who is sent on a special diplomatic mission

Three days and nights my business forced me to lodge and mix with the bloody Pequot ambassadors, whose hands and arms, methought, reeked with the blood of my countrymen, . . . and from whom I could not but nightly look for their bloody knives at my own throat also. God wondrously preserved me, and helped me to break to pieces the Pequot's negotiation and design; and to make and finish . . . the English league with the Narragansetts and Mohegans against the Pequots.

In this engraving from the 1630s, Roger Williams, acting as a negotiator for Massachusetts Bay Colony, speaks to Pequot leaders in an effort to prevent an Indian alliance that could destroy the English settlements.

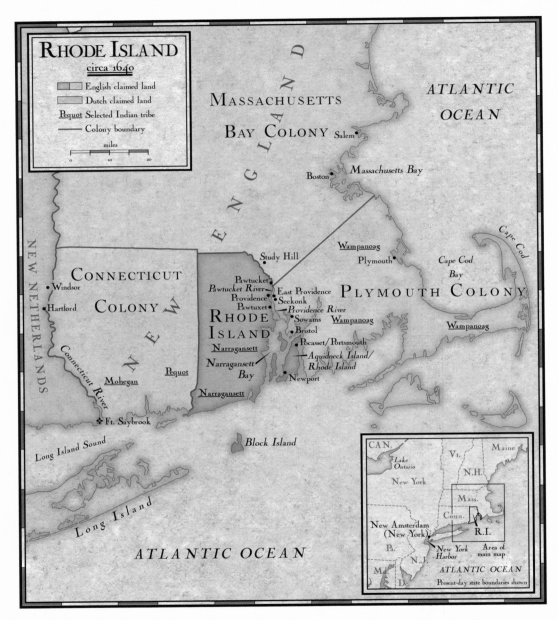

RHODE ISLAND
circa 1640

English claimed land
Dutch claimed land
Pequot Selected Indian tribe
Colony boundary

miles

0   10   20

MASSACHUSETTS BAY COLONY Salem•

ATLANTIC OCEAN

Boston• *Massachusetts Bay*

Cape Cod

NEW NETHERLANDS

NEW ENGLAND

Study Hill• *Wampanoag* Plymouth• *Cape Cod Bay*

CONNECTICUT COLONY

Windsor•

Hartford•

Pawtucket•
Pawtucket River •East Providence
Providence• •Seekonk
Pawtuxet• •*Providence River* **PLYMOUTH COLONY**
•Sowams *Wampanoag*
RHODE ISLAND •Bristol
•Pocasset/Portsmouth *Wampanoag*
Narragansett •—*Aquidneck Island/*
Narragansett Bay *Rhode Island*
Mohegan• *Pequot* Newport•
Narragansett

Connecticut River

⚹Ft. Saybrook

Long Island Sound

Block Island

Long Island

ATLANTIC OCEAN

CAN.
Lake Ontario Vt. Maine
New York N.H.
Mass.
Conn.
New Amsterdam (New York)• R.I.
Pa. •New York Harbor Area of main map
N.J.
Md. De. *ATLANTIC OCEAN*
Present-day state boundaries shown

This map shows the British colonies in New England around 1640. At that time, most of the land bordering the western shores of Narragansett Bay belonged to the Narragansett people. Plymouth Colony, homeland of the Wampanoag, claimed lands bordering the eastern shores of the bay. The first settlements in what would become known as Rhode Island were concentrated along the Seekonk and Providence Rivers and on Aquidneck Island.

The war raged for two years, while Williams continued to serve the Bay Colony by acting as an interpreter for the English and their new Narragansett allies. He even relayed important information from the Narragansett about how the English could beat the Pequot, making his work vital to the English victory in 1638.

PROVIDENCE

During the Pequot War, Williams was busy in Providence. His work there was guided by the beliefs that had caused him to be banished from Massachusetts. During the winter of 1636, before founding Providence, Williams had asked permission of the sachems Canonicus and Miantonomi to settle some land. The sachems gave him the large piece of land that included Providence, in addition to land in the north, called Pawtucket (see map page 32). Because Roger Williams gave the sachems gifts in return, it is often said that he "bought" Providence. However, Williams himself said, *"I never got anything out of Canonicus but by gift."*

As more and more people left Massachusetts colonies to seek religious freedom in Providence, it became clear that the settlers would need some form of government. After thinking about how to create a government that allowed people the freedom to believe whatever they wanted, Williams asked the settlers to sign an agreement.

✕✕✕✕✕✕✕✕✕✕ P R O F I L E ✕✕✕✕✕✕✕✕✕✕

William Blackstone

A man named William Blackstone, a Church of England minister, was the first European to live in what would become Rhode Island.

He had become unhappy with how the church was run. He joined an expedition to settle New England in 1623 and began living north of Plymouth Colony, near what is now Beacon Hill in Boston. Blackstone spent his time reading and planting an apple orchard. He succeeded in cultivating a now famous kind of apple called Yellow Sweetings.

When the Puritans arrived in 1630, Blackstone invited them to settle nearby and gave them a large part of his land. However, when Blackstone learned of the Puritans' intolerance for anyone who did not agree with their religious beliefs, he decided that he could not remain. *"I left England to get from under the power of the Lord Bishops but in America I am fallen under the power of the Lord Brethren,"* he said, explaining that the Puritans were no more tolerant than Anglican England.

Blackstone settled near the Pawtucket River, about 10 miles (16 km) north of Providence. He built a home he called Study Hill, because of its large library, and planted an apple orchard. Study Hill became part of Rhode Island in 1746, when it became the town of Cumberland.

According to this agreement, there was no governor or other single person in charge of the settlement. Instead, the family heads met every two weeks to discuss rules and make decisions that affected the colony's welfare, such as where and what crops to plant and how to provide security from wild animals. The government could not make rules about religion. The agreement was remarkable because it clearly defined the separation of church and state in government.

The families that followed Williams to Providence began to get nervous about their claim to the land. They wanted a document from the Narragansett sachems to confirm their gift of land to Roger Williams. Williams wrote out this document in 1637, and Canonicus and Miantonomi signed it by placing an X next to their names. But that was not the end of the matter. As far as the Providence families could tell from this agreement, Roger Williams owned all the colony's lands. They persuaded Williams to draft another document stating that he shared the land in Providence with them. The land in Pawtucket served as a common grazing land for the settlement's livestock. By 1638, more than 20 families and single men lived along the Providence River.

CHAPTER THREE

The Settlement on Aquidneck

OUTCAST ANNE HUTCHINSON *settles Aquidneck.*
Rhode Island's new towns grow as settlers plant crops and
expand their towns.

 oger Williams was not the only person to be banished from Massachusetts Bay Colony for not conforming to the Puritan society there. Outcasts founded the first four towns in Rhode Island. Shortly after Williams settled at Providence, a group forced out of Massachusetts Bay in 1638 founded

OPPOSITE: Anne Hutchinson is shown preaching in her house in Boston in this 1901 illustration by artist Howard Pyle. Hutchinson's weekly meetings would draw more than 50 people eager to hear her comments on the sermons given by local preachers.

another town to the south on Aquidneck Island in Narragansett Bay. This town was called Pocasset. The controversy that led to its founding revolved around a woman named Anne Hutchinson.

Anne Hutchinson was married to a merchant named William Hutchinson. In England, these devout Puritans followed the teachings of the Reverend John Cotton. When Cotton left England for Boston in 1633, Anne and William, with their eight children, followed him, arriving in 1634.

Anne Hutchinson was a skillful nurse and a midwife, who knew so much about medicine that some called her a physician. Soon after arriving in Boston, Hutchinson began to hold weekly women's meetings at her home. At these meetings, she would relay the previous Sunday's sermon to the women whose household duties prevented them from going to church. Because she was very familiar with the Bible, she would also explain and comment on the sermon.

midwife—a person, usually a woman, who is trained to assist women in childbirth

The number of people coming to Hutchinson's weekly meetings increased as she gained a reputation for holding lively discussions. Men even began attending her meetings. One of her admirers said, *"I'll bring you to a woman who preaches better gospel than any of your black-coats [priests] who have been at the ninnyversity* [satirical word for university], *a woman of another kind of spirit."* Soon she began teaching her own ideas, even criticizing some Puritan doctrines.

Hutchinson and her followers became known as anti-nomians, which means "against laws." They were not in favor of getting rid of all religious laws, but they believed that it was not necessary for a person to strictly follow the Bible's laws to gain salvation, or deliverance from sin. Hutchinson said, *"As I understand it, laws, commands, rules, and edicts are for those who have not the light which makes plain the pathway."*

By 1637, Hutchinson's meetings had grown very large. The governor of Massachusetts Bay, John Winthrop, began punishing the antinomians. Many were fined or lost their right to vote. Some of Hutchinson's followers were even banished from the colony.

In November 1637, the magistrates placed Anne Hutchinson on trial for disturbing the peace with her meetings and ideas. On the first day, she testified so skillfully that her accusers could not convict her. On the second day of her trial, Hutchinson gave a long speech. She claimed "inward revelations," or a direct communication from God, and quoted the Bible. The court used these claims against her, saying they went directly against Puritan teachings. Hutchinson was found guilty and banished. The Reverend John Wilson delivered the sentence: *"In the name of the Lord Jesus Christ and in the name of the church I do not only pronounce you worthy to be cast out I do cast you out; . . . therefore I command you in the name of Christ Jesus and of his church as a leper to withdraw yourself out of the congregation."*

A colonial family is banished from Massachusetts Bay by Puritan leaders who were intolerant of anyone who did not follow their strict teachings. The family was forced to leave quickly with few possessions.

Hutchinson's many followers had not been idle all this time. In 1637, they had begun making plans to leave Massachusetts and settle somewhere else. Dr. John Clarke and a rich merchant named William Coddington were chosen to select a site for the new colony. At first the men began searching to the north of Massachusetts, but the harsh winter weather drove them off. In early 1638, Clarke and Coddington traveled south, intending to go to Long Island, off the southern shore of Connecticut. Instead, they found a much closer location with the help of Roger Williams. Dr. Clarke wrote:

"So to a town called Providence we came, which was begun by one Mr. Roger Williams (who for a matter of conscience had not long before been exiled from [Massachusetts]), by whom we were courteously and lovingly received, and with whom we advised about our [plan]. He readily presented two places before us on the same Narragansett Bay, the one upon the [mainland] called Sowams, the other called then Aquidneck, now [the island of] Rhode Island.

It turned out that the place called Sowams (probably near Bristol) was claimed by Plymouth Colony. So Aquidneck Island, which was later renamed Rhode Island, was decided upon as the site for the new colony. In March 1638, Roger Williams went to his friend Miantonomi, a sachem of the Narragansett, to obtain a deed to the island for the new settlers. He wrote, *"It was not . . . money that could have purchased Rhode Island. Rhode Island was obtained by love; by the love and favor which . . . [I] had with that great Sachem Miantonomi, about the league which I procured between the Massachusetts English . . . and the Narragansetts in the Pequot War."*

Clarke and Coddington returned to Boston with the good news in early March. By this time, Anne Hutchinson had been banished, along with 75 of her followers. On March 7, 1638, just before the group left Boston, the people signed an agreement, now called the Portsmouth Compact, which set up new settlements. There would be freedom of worship, but only for Protestants. William Coddington was elected to be the group's first leader.

The first settlement was established in a cove on the north end of Aquidneck Island. It was called Pocasset for the first two years until the name was changed to Portsmouth. The land was divided among the settlers. Unlike Providence's beginnings, the town of Portsmouth was planned out. An inn, a brewery, and a general grocery store were built, *"to sell wines and strong waters and such necessary provisions as may be useful."* A jail was built also. Crops such as corn and beans were planted and watched carefully to make sure they were not damaged by animals. To keep everything clean, cattle and pigs were kept 6 miles (10 km) out of town.

In April 1639, a group of people led by William Coddington and John Clarke left Pocasset and moved to the south end of the island. Historians remain unsure about their reason for leaving. It may have been because of an argument over how the colony should be governed. But the decision may also have been made because the island's southern end had a natural harbor. The people who stayed at Pocasset signed a new compact, agreeing to abide by the laws of England's King Charles. They elected William Hutchinson to be judge for a term of one year.

Coddington, Clarke, and the others who left Pocasset went on to found a town called Newport. At first, they lived in tents and wigwams, but they soon built sturdier dwellings. Dr. Clarke built the first Baptist church in America in Newport and served as its minister. (At the time,

Baptists were a group of Christians whose beliefs were very similar to the Puritans'.) Coddington was elected judge of Newport, serving with three assistants for a year.

EARLY LIFE

The first settlers lived busy lives full of hard work with very little comfort. Providence's first settlers built log cabins, using a simple hand ax to flatten two sides of each log. On Aquidneck, the

John Clarke, minister of the Baptist Church in Newport, is featured in a painting titled "Portrait of a Clergyman," by artist Guillam de Ville, made in the late 1650s.

settlers of both towns may have brought cut lumber from the Bay Colony with them. As early as 1639, they established a sawmill on the island to produce more lumber. Their houses were simple, with only one or two rooms.

The settlers had to grow and catch their own food. Farming was the most common job; all the first settlers received farmland to grow corn and beans. Although the soil on Aquidneck was very good for growing crops, the land around Providence was hard and rocky. The settlers there used a technique learned from the Indians. They would plant their corn with a fish just underneath it. The fish provided extra nutrients to the soil.

A member of the Patuxet tribe is shown teaching a group of Englishmen how to enrich the soil where they plant corn by placing a fish in the ground to serve as fertilizer.

Besides the crops they harvested, the settlers ate fish and shellfish, like lobsters and a kind of clam called a quahog, from the bay. The settlers hunted turkey, deer, and other wild animals. Berries and nuts grew in the area, too, so the settlers had a varied diet. Most foods were boiled and seasoned with salt or maple sugar. Another popular way of cooking was to simply put a bunch of ingredients in a single pot and stew them. This was sometimes called succotash, and although there were many different ways to make it, it usually combined corn, lima beans, and pork.

In March 1640, Portsmouth and Newport were united under a single government, run by a governor, a deputy governor, and four assistants. The governor and two assistants were chosen from one town, while the deputy and two assistants came from the other.

As the towns grew, many of the original settlers moved on to new places. When William Hutchinson died in 1642, Anne Hutchinson and her children moved from Portsmouth to Pelham Bay on Long Island Sound, where she was murdered by a band of Delaware Indians in 1643.

CHAPTER FOUR

Becoming a Colony

MASSACHUSETTS BAY COLONY sees an opportunity to expand its influence with the arrival of Samuel Gorton. Roger Williams obtains a charter uniting the Rhode Island settlements under the Incorporation of Providence Plantations.

n the early 1640s, Massachusetts Bay was growing and wanted to claim land on nearby Narragansett Bay (the "Narragansett Country"). This desire to expand led to decades of argument over borders between Rhode Island and its neighbors, Massachusetts and Connecticut. The Indians still used the land, and it had not yet been claimed by Europeans. Further, the English government had not yet officially

OPPOSITE: Settlers on the island of Aquidneck chase a farmer's cattle off land in dispute. The man in a black cape is holding a piece of paper which may be a deed showing ownership of the land.

recognized the settlements at Providence and on Aquidneck by issuing a charter. This meant that Massachusetts Bay could claim the land near these settlements. The Bay Colony's best opportunity to settle the Narragansett Country came about 1644, when a preacher named Samuel Gorton arrived from England.

PROBLEMS WITH THE NEIGHBORS

Samuel Gorton's ideas were unpopular with the strict Puritans. He preached that people did not need ministers to know God and that English laws should apply to the settlements and colonies in America. He came to Boston in March 1637, hoping *"to enjoy liberty of conscience in respect to faith towards God, and for no other end"* and moved to Plymouth Colony almost immediately.

Gorton soon found himself in trouble. In 1638, a maid in Gorton's house was caught "smiling in congregation" and was threatened with banishment. Gorton went to court to defend her, but ended up being fined and banished from the colony in the middle of a raging blizzard. Gorton, along with some people who agreed with his ideas, traveled to the Narragansett Bay area.

Gorton arrived in Pocasset shortly before Coddington and the others left to start Newport. In 1640, when the two towns united, Gorton's belief in English law made him question whether a colony could create a government at all without the king's permission. His opinion made Gorton unpopular with the colony officials, and he soon moved on from Pocasset.

Next, Gorton tried to settle at Providence. Roger Williams wrote in a letter to Governor Winthrop that "*Master Gorton, having foully abused high and low at Aquidneck, is now bewitching and bemaddening poor Providence . . . with his unclean and foul censures of all the ministers of this country.*" Williams did not like Gorton because Gorton had questioned the right of the colonists to create a government on Aquidneck. Williams also disagreed with many of Gorton's religious ideas.

Despite Williams's tolerance for different religious ideas, he was not as open-minded about matters of government. In a famous letter, Williams compared government to a ship:

> *the commander of the ship ought to command the ship's course; yea, and command also that justice, peace, and sobriety, be kept and practiced, both among the seamen and the passengers . . . if any refuse to obey the common laws and orders of the ship . . . if any should write or preach there should be no commander because all are equal in Christ . . . the commander . . . may judge . . . and punish such transgressors.*

In 1642, Gorton and his followers bought some land in a place called Pawtuxet, about 5 miles (8 km) south of

Providence. Here, they met the Arnold family, led by William Arnold and his son Benedict, who had sold land for people to build homes. This purchase did not include enough land for the people's cattle to graze. When someone's cows grazed on the land the Arnolds had kept for themselves, they impounded the cows until the owners paid to get them back. The Arnolds wanted the Gortonites to leave and, in order to get rid of them, asked Massachusetts for help.

impound—to seize and hold

The Bay Colony was very interested in claiming some land on Narragansett Bay, because of its good location for trading with both Indians and other European colonies. In 1643, William Arnold wrote to the Bay Colony, accusing Gorton of "riotous" and "uncivil" conduct.

Together with 12 other families, Gorton moved a few miles farther south. They bought a piece of land called Shawomet from Miantonomi. Massachusetts Bay claimed Shawomet for itself, however, and Gorton was charged with trespassing. Colony officials, along with 40 armed guards, went to Shawomet to bring Gorton back. As the small army neared Shawomet, the officials received a letter from Gorton, saying "If you present a gun, make haste to give first fire: for we are come to put fire on the earth, and it is our desire to have it speedily kindled." The Bay Colony officials responded with an offer to talk things over. But if the Gortonites did not give up, they would be treated "as men prepared for slaughter."

An attack began on October 8, 1643. The Gortonites held out for more than a week while the Bay Colony soldiers shot at their barricade and tried to set fire to it. The Gortonites hardly fired a shot, only *"at random and in the night, to keep them from working their trenches near unto us."*

The Gortonites, attempting to escape from Massachusetts Bay Colony soldiers, wade into the sea to board a boat to take them to safety.

Finally, the soldiers captured the Gortonites, but only by making false promises. Gorton, who wanted to prevent any deaths, agreed that they would go to Boston, but only as free men. The captain of the soldiers agreed, but once the Gortonites came out of hiding, they were seized and locked in chains. Their cattle were taken, and they were stripped of all valuables.

Boston magistrates placed Gorton and the other men on trial, not for trespassing on land that Massachusetts Bay now claimed, but for heresy. Gorton was tried for his religious beliefs, which differed from strict Puritan teachings. The Gortonites were put in prison and forced to work for the Bay Colony for a year while imprisoned.

heresy—an opinion or a doctrine that differs with established religious beliefs

The DEATH *of* MIANTONOMI

IN MAY 1643, THE COLONIES of Massachusetts Bay, Plymouth, Connecticut, and New Haven formed the United Colonies of New England, with the purpose of settling boundary disputes, coordinating defenses, and diminishing the power of the Native Americans in the region. There had been rumors of an Indian revolt, and the colonies were scared. The Providence and Aquidneck settlements  asked to be included in the federation, but they were refused because the other colonies disapproved of the religious freedom the settlers enjoyed.

The United Colonies made a treaty with Uncas, the chief Mohegan sachem. When the Mohegan attacked and killed some of the Narragansett, Miantonomi led a counterattack. He was captured by Uncas, who brought Miantonomi to United Colony officials in Boston. The Bay Colony was not happy with Miantonomi for selling land to Gorton. Rather than kill Miantonomi themselves, they turned him over to Uncas with instructions to kill Miantonomi without torture. Two Englishmen were present when Uncas carried out the sentence with a hatchet to the back of Miantonomi's head.

BECOMING A COLONY

Concerned by Massachusetts Bay's seizure of the Gortonites land, Rhode Island colonists acted quickly. In 1643, Roger Williams was chosen to travel to England to obtain a royal charter for the Providence and Aquidneck settlements. This would prevent a takeover by the Bay Colony.

When Williams arrived in England in 1643, the country was in the midst of a civil war, and King Charles I had fled from London. Williams was forced to appeal to Parliament for the charter. With the help of his friend Sir Henry Vane, Williams was successful. The charter was issued on March 14, 1644.

The charter that Williams received created a common civil government for the three existing settlements, which were now united and named the Incorporation of Providence Plantations (known as Providence Plantations). It granted the people *"full power and authority to rule themselves . . . by such a form of civil government as by voluntary consent of all, or the greater part of them, [that] they shall find most suitable to their estate and condition; . . . provided . . . that the laws . . . be conformable to the laws of England so far as the nature and constitution of the place will allow."*

By the time Roger Williams returned with the new charter in 1644, Samuel Gorton and his followers had been released by Massachusetts. Gorton returned to Aquidneck. His previous banishment from the area was revoked because he had already served time in prison for his views. In the summer of 1645, Massachusetts Bay and Plymouth challenged the charter that Roger Williams had received in England. Another trip to England would be needed in order to make sure the charter was not withdrawn. Gorton, now very popular as an advocate of religious freedom, made that trip with two other men.

A Key into the
LANGUAGES
OF AMERICA

DURING HIS VOYAGE TO ENGLAND IN 1643, ROGER WILLIAMS wrote a dictionary of the New England Indians' languages, called *A Key into the Languages of America*. He wrote the guide *"as a private help to my own memory, so that I might not . . . lose what I had so dearly bought in some years' hardship . . . among the Barbarians [non-Christians]."* The book contained more than languages, since Williams included his own observations about the Indians, their lives, and their culture. He even added little poems, like this one, which explained that the Indians were not inferior to Europeans:

Boast not proud English, of thy birth and blood.
Thy brother Indian is of birth as good.
Through God's grace, some Englishmen might yet see,
Heaven ope[n] to Indian wild, But shut to thee.

At that time Williams' belief that Native Americans were not savages was unusual.

Their quest was successful. The Parliamentary Governor for Foreign Plantations, the Earl of Warwick, confirmed that Williams's charter was valid and added the lands of Shawomet to it. The earl further ordered that Massachusetts Bay return Shawomet to its owners, the Gortonites. The Gortonite families, who had been living on Aquidneck, returned to Shawomet. In gratitude to the earl who made it possible, they renamed the place Warwick.

On landing in Boston, Samuel Gorton presents an official order from the Earl of Warwick that forbids any interference with Gorton's safe return to Rhode Island.

THE CHARTER OF 1663

With the end of the English Civil War in 1660 and a new king, Charles II, on the throne, the Providence Plantations had reason to worry again about the validity of their charter. It was quickly decided that the settlers should try to get a royal charter from the new king. In 1661, the colony wrote to minister Dr. John Clarke, who was in England at the time, to represent them to the king and his council and to seek a royal charter from the king.

Clarke wrote two letters to the king's council, containing lots of praise and flattery for Charles II. Clarke wrote about the people of Rhode Island. He said they, *"have it much in their hearts . . . to hold forth a lively experiment, that a flourishing civil state may . . . best be maintained . . . with a full liberty in religious concernments."* Clarke's efforts succeeded, and a new royal charter was issued on July 8, 1663, proclaiming the settlements listed in the document as now part of Rhode Island. It was the most liberal charter granted to any English colony.

The charter established the Colony of Rhode Island and Providence Plantations, and safeguarded the religious liberty of Rhode Islanders by declaring that *"no person within the colony . . . shall be [in any way] . . . punished . . . for any differences in opinion in matters of religion, [so long as they] do not actually disturb the civil peace of [the] colony. . . . Every person may . . . freely and fully have and enjoy his own judgments and consciences, in matters of religious concernment."* The charter also outlined the government of the colony, which would consist of a governor, deputy governor, and at least ten assistants. These ten would be elected, some from each town. The elected assistants were called the General Assembly, and it created laws, penalties for breaking them, and courts. It set the boundaries of towns, trade with the Indians, and created a militia.

When the charter arrived in Rhode Island in November 1663, it was read aloud to all the people assembled at Newport and *"with much gravity held up on high, and presented to the perfect view of all the people."* ❋

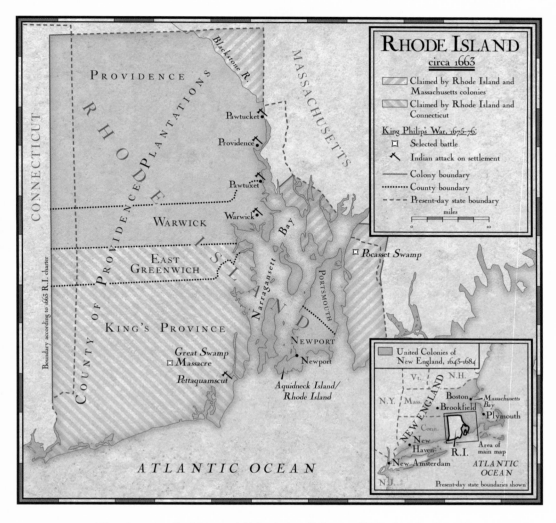

RHODE ISLAND
circa 1663

Claimed by Rhode Island and Massachusetts colonies

Claimed by Rhode Island and Connecticut

King Philip's War, 1675-76:

□ Selected battle

✕ Indian attack on settlement

Colony boundary

County boundary

Present-day state boundary

miles

0   10

CONNECTICUT

PROVIDENCE

RHODE

Blackstone R.

MASSACHUSETTS

Pawtucket

Providence

Pawtuxet

Warwick

WARWICK

Narragansett Bay

Portsmouth

EAST GREENWICH

Boundary according to 1663 R.I. charter

COUNTY OF PROVIDENCE PLANTATIONS

ISLAND

KING'S PROVINCE

Great Swamp Massacre

Pettaquamscut

□ Pocasset Swamp

NEWPORT

Newport

Aquidneck Island/ Rhode Island

ATLANTIC OCEAN

United Colonies of New England, 1643-1684

Vt.   N.H.

N.Y.   Mass.   Boston   Massachusetts Bay

Conn.   Brookfield   Plymouth

New England

New Haven

R.I.   Area of main map

New Amsterdam   ATLANTIC OCEAN

N.J.

Present-day state boundaries shown

The charter of 1663 established the Colony of Rhode Island and Providence Plantations. At the time, Rhode Island was the new name for Aquidneck Island, which included the settlements of Portsmouth in the north and Newport in the South. Providence Plantations was made up of Providence, Warwick, and East Greenwich as well as King's Province, formerly known as Narragansett Country. Surrounded by the United Colonies (see inset map), Rhode Island faced challenges from Connecticut on its western boundary and from the Massachusetts colonies in the east.

CHAPTER FIVE

Decline of Relations with the Indians

QUAKERS SETTLE IN RHODE ISLAND. *King Philip's War all but destroys the Native population in the Narragansett region.*

eligious freedom was very important to the founders of Rhode Island. The extent of the freedom enjoyed in the young colony was far greater than anywhere else in the colonies and even surpassed the freedoms found in Britain and other countries in

OPPOSITE: Wampanoag chief Metacom, also known as King Philip, poses in a feathered headdress, holding a musket. King Philip waged war, unsuccessfully, against English colonists to hold on to Native American lands and culture.

Europe. The kind of freedom given by the charter of 1663 was almost unheard of. Over the years, Rhode Island became a haven for the persecuted. The first, most influential of these groups was the Quakers.

THE QUAKERS

A man named George Fox started the Religious Society of Friends in England about 1652. Fox began preaching that people did not need a church or even a minister to worship God. Like Anne Hutchinson, he believed that people could be in direct communication with God.

The people who gathered around Fox shared his beliefs. Their worship services did not have a minister or anyone else in charge. They would meet in someone's home and sit silently in a circle. There were no rituals, like planned prayers or hymns. Whenever people felt "moved by the Spirit," they would stand up and speak or sing. They came to be called the "Quakers" because their prayers were accompanied by a lot of shaking and moving. They placed great importance on truthfulness and non-violence. The Quakers practiced passive resistance. They also believed that all human beings were equal. For this reason, they would not yield to those with a higher social standing, as was the custom of the time. For example, they would not remove their hats as a sign of respect.

passive resistance— nonviolent methods of protest, such as peaceful demonstrations or fasting

The first Quakers came to New England in July 1656. They landed at Boston, where they were immediately jailed for their beliefs by the Puritans. Their literature was burned, and they were soon banished. The Rhode Island General Assembly noted that *"they delight to be persecuted by civil powers, and when they are so, they are like to gain more adherents . . . by their patient sufferings."*

Quaker leader George Fox (standing on chair) preaches in a tavern in this painting by E. Wehnert. At his feet lies a young woman, exhausted by prayer.

Mary Dyer

Mary Dyer, a Quaker, was born in England in 1651. In 1658, she was expelled from Massachusetts for preaching Quaker teachings in Boston. Four times she returned and was arrested before she and two Quaker men were sentenced to be hanged.

Dyer's son begged the Bay Colony for mercy and gained her release, but the Puritan officials did not tell her right away. Instead, they led her and the other two Quakers to Boston Commons. They placed the noose around her neck, and she watched as the two others were hanged. Puritan officials tried to get her to repent and give up her beliefs, but she refused. So they banished her from Massachusetts again and ordered her not to return on pain of death. After she was released, Dyer said, *"with wicked hands have you put two of them to death, which makes me feel that the mercies of the wicked is cruelty."*

In defiance of the order, Mary Dyer returned to Boston in May 1660. This time, she went to the gallows. She said, *"in obedience to the will of the Lord God I came, and in his will I abide faithful to the death."* King Charles, after receiving reports of what was happening in Massachusetts Bay, ordered that the colony stop executing and persecuting Quakers.

This 18th-century painting of a Quaker meeting shows a Quaker's hat flying off his head as he prays aloud. Members of this religious group were called Quakers because they would often shake with emotion while praying.

Quaker missionaries traveling from England arrived in Newport in the fall of 1657 aboard the *Woodhouse*, which had been turned away from the Dutch settlement of New Amsterdam (now New York City). They were welcomed in Rhode Island, and within a few years Quakers had become an important group in the colony. Many people joined the Society of Friends, and its members frequently served in the colony's government.

Massachusetts Bay was determined to keep the Quakers from preaching their ideas to its citizens. In September 1657, Massachusetts, calling the Quakers *"dangerous pests,"* demanded that Rhode Island *"remove those Quakers that have been received, and for the future prohibit their comings among you."* But Rhode Island, founded on and committed to the ideal of religious freedom, refused the demands of its neighbor, and the Bay Colony had no authority to force Rhode Island to comply. Rhode Island's governor replied, *"we have no law among us whereby to punish any [person] for only declaring by words, their minds and understandings concerning the things and ways of God, as to salvation and an eternal condition."*

As Rhode Island grew, other groups of persecuted people arrived. The lands around Providence and Warwick were divided up in the 1670s, forming new towns. One of these, East Greenwich, was settled in 1686 by the Huguenots, a group of French Protestants driven out of their Catholic country. Rhode Island also welcomed Jews as early as the 1650s.

KING PHILIP'S WAR

By the early 1670s, Roger Williams's friendship with the local Indian tribes had contributed to almost 40 years of peace between the Indians and the colonists in Massachusetts, Plymouth, and Rhode Island. But that peace was about to be shattered by a brutal, bloody war. The great sachems that Williams had befriended were dead by 1675. Canonicus's son Canonchet was now chief sachem of the Narragansett. Massasoit's son Metacomet had been named Philip by the English when he was young. In 1662, Philip became sachem of the Wampanoag, and for years he watched as the English in Massachusetts Bay and Plymouth pushed his tribe farther west. The rapid expansion of the English colonies convinced Philip that Indian and Englishman could not live peacefully together. The Natives were losing their lands and their way of life. *"I am determined not to live till I have no country,"* said Philip.

King Philip began to prepare for war. He hoped other tribes in the area, especially the Narragansett in Rhode Island, would form an alliance with him against the English. Fighting began in 1675, when Wampanoag Indians killed some cattle grazing near their tribal lands around present-day Bristol, Rhode Island. An angry farmer responded by killing an Indian brave. King Philip's War had begun.

brave—a Native American warrior

Over the summer and fall of 1675, fierce battles were fought throughout towns in the Bay Colony, Plymouth, and Connecticut. Tribes throughout the region terrorized colonists living in these areas. Philip was rumored to be working for an alliance with the Narragansett in Rhode Island.

The United Colonies sent a thousand soldiers to Rhode Island to attack the Narragansett and prevent them from joining forces with King Philip and his Wampanoag warriors. As the troops from Massachusetts marched through the Rhode Island towns of Providence and Warwick, volunteers joined them. Acting on information provided by a Narragansett traitor, the soldiers found the Indians' winter camp on an island in the middle of a big swamp.

On December 19, 1675, the colonial forces moved into position to attack. The Indians had built a stockade on the island, but it was not complete. The battle, which has become known as the Great Swamp Massacre, was fierce, and both sides suffered losses, but the Indians had the worst of it. When a weak spot in the stockade was found, the Indians inside were massacred.

An illustration of the Great Swamp Massacre near present-day West Kingston, Rhode Island, shows the English colonial forces using a fallen tree as a bridge to cross the water surrounding the Narragansett camp. Smoke from muskets fired by both sides fills the air.

A Soldier's Account of the
GREAT SWAMP MASSACRE

THIS LETTER, WRITTEN BY AN UNIDENTIFIED ENGLISH SOLDIER, details the horror of the fight in the swamp.

We marched through the snow and came to a thick swamp wherein were encamped 3500 Indians. We first demanded to have Philip and his Adherents to be delivered [as] pris‑ oners to us . . . and had no other answer but shot; then we [set fire to] about 500 wigwams, and killed all that we met with of them, as well Squaws and Papooses (i.e. Women and Children) as Sanups (i. e. Men). In the midst of the wood . . . the Indians had built a fort; the stone‑wall whereof enclosed about four or five acres, in which rampart was about 1000 Indians. . . .

We were no sooner entered the fort, but our enemies began to fly, and ours had now a carnage rather than a fight. . . . This fight and execution continued from three a clock in the afternoon till night.

The soldier wrote that the troops killed about 500 Indian warriors, not counting *"women and children the number of which we took no account of."* He gives the number of wounded and dead English at 207.

Canonchet and some of his tribe escaped the massacre. After a long march through Connecticut, they were able to join up with the remaining Wampanoag in Massachusetts Bay. Historians call this journey the "hunger march," because the colonists had destroyed the Indians' stores of food.

Although there were fewer Indian attacks during the winter, some towns were not spared. Warwick, Rhode Island, was totally burned down, except for one stone house, and in March 1676, more than 50 houses in Providence were destroyed. Some people, known to be friends of the Indians, were saved. In Providence, one of the Indians told Roger Williams, *"you are a good man; you have been kind to us many years; not a hair of your head shall be touched."*

Roger Williams's friendship with Rhode Island's Narragansett in the mid 1600s eventually guaranteed his safety during King Philip's War.

Shortly after the attack on Providence, Canonchet and his party were surprised by a force of Connecticut troops and their Mohegan allies at the Wampanoag's main camp on the Connecticut River. Canonchet, who refused to order his Narragansett warriors to lay down their weapons, was killed by the English. Before he died, he said, "[I like] it well that [I] should die before [my] heart is soft or [I have] spoken words unworthy of [myself]." The rest of the Native Americans were slaughtered in battle or drowned in the river trying to escape.

Despite orders from Philip to wage counterattacks, Indian forces were sparse, and the alliances soon crumbled. Philip traveled back to his camp at Swansea in Massachusetts Bay Colony, where the war had started. He was found and killed by the English in August 1676. Much property in Rhode Island had been destroyed, but not many Rhode Islanders were killed because they had fled to Aquidneck and the other islands for safety. With the power of the local Indians broken and the tribal population much smaller, Rhode Islanders would be free to spread out and settle throughout the Narragansett Country south and west of Providence.

CHAPTER SIX

Life and Growth in the Early 18th Century

IMPORTANT PORT TOWNS DEVELOP *in Rhode Island*
as the colony prospers.

he end of the 17th century saw real growth in the little colony of Rhode Island. More towns were created: East Greenwich (carved out of Warwick), Westerly and Kingstown (both in the south), and New Shoreham on Block Island. In the mid-18th century (between 1723 and 1765) 14 more towns were created, each one carved out of prior towns. Providence and

OPPOSITE: The first cotton mill in America was established at Pawtucket along the Blackstone River by Samuel Slater in the late 1700s. Rhode Islanders stand alongside the great river's falls that power the mill.

Newport became busy port cities, where people could become rich through trade.

A BUSTLING PORT

By the first few years of the 18th century, all the land on Aquidneck had been divided into farms. With little land left to purchase, people turned to industries supported by the port cities. Shipbuilding soon became an important industry in Newport. From 1700 to 1710, more than a hundred ships were built there. Trading became the primary occupation in Newport.

Prominent Rhode Island merchants and sea captains are among the crowd in this tavern scene titled "Sea Captains Carousing in Surinam," painted by American artist John Greenwood in 1758. Many Rhode Islanders became wealthy trading with the Dutch colony in South America in spite of British laws prohibiting such commerce.

The Newport merchants shipped the items produced in Rhode Island to other colonies and places like Jamaica, the Bahamas, and the Bermudas. Lumber, horses, butter, and cheese were exchanged for molasses and sugar in Barbados. Cotton, salt, cocoa, and iron were among the other imports.

PRIVATEERS

Between 1651 and 1763, Britain fought many wars with the Dutch, French, and Spanish. During this time, many Rhode Islanders took to the sea, because there was great wealth to be made through privateering.

Privateers were privately owned ships, armed with cannon and soldiers, commissioned by a colony's government to attack and capture enemy vessels. The captured ships and their cargoes, called prizes, were then sold for profits that would go to the owners, officers, and crew of the privateer.

Sometimes, captains would attack ships without permission from a government, thus becoming pirates. Nathaniel Coddington, a member of the Court of the Admiralty (the governing body regulating shipping in the colony), said "*All the vessels had great arms mounted; no cost was spared for small arms and powder. . . . The discourse was generally that they were bound for Madagascar, but some [thought] they were to go to the Red Sea where the money was as plenty as stones and sand, saying the people there were infidels, and it was no sin to kill them.*" Rhode Island was home to many famous privateers and pirates.

Thomas Tew

Thomas Tew was captain of a ship called the *Amity*. In 1694, he applied for a privateer's commission from Governor John Easton. Easton denied him, even after Tew tried to bribe the governor. Tew sailed anyway. He became a pirate and attacked ships off the coast of Africa. He created a small colony of pirates on the island of Madagascar and used it as a base of operations. A crewman reported on a typical mission: *"Steering for Surat [a city in India] we caught up with one of the ships which we took after she had fired three shots, she had 50,000 or 60,000 [pounds] on board in silver and gold. We shortly afterwards spied another ship, mounting forty guns and carrying (as was said) 800 men. She stood a fight of three hours and yielded."* It was said that Tew eventually returned to Newport and repaid the owners of his ship 14 times their original investment.

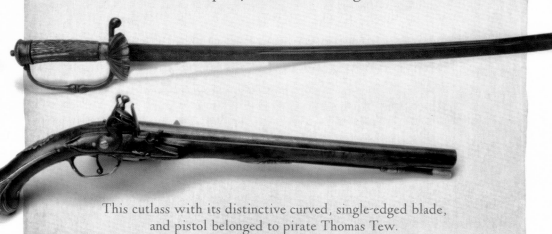

This cutlass with its distinctive curved, single-edged blade, and pistol belonged to pirate Thomas Tew.

British authorities viewed Rhode Island as *"the most piratical in the King's Dominions."* Lord Bellomont, sent to the Colonies to stop the piracy, wrote, *"I am well informed what constant encouragement [Rhode Islanders] give to pirates to come in there, and bring in their spoils."* Despite the government's efforts to suppress privateers and pirates, the practice continued even during the Revolutionary War.

RHODE ISLAND AND THE SLAVE TRADE

Although privateering was very profitable, it was nothing compared with the slave trade. At the turn of the 18th century, the slave trade was highly profitable. In Newport, the slave trade brought so much wealth that it helped start a "golden age," when great mansions were built and arts and literature flourished.

The slave trade was supplied by ships making three separate voyages, so it became known as the triangle trade. In Newport and other Rhode Island towns, molasses and sugar from the West Indies were turned into rum. The rum was loaded up and sent to Africa. There, ships sailed along the coast, trading the rum for slaves in many different places. The slaves were usually either prisoners taken in battle by rival villages or people who had committed a crime. With chains around their neck and ankles, slaves were packed into a space between a ship's decks. The space was a little more than 3 feet (1 meter) high. When about a hundred men, women, and children had been bought, the ship began the "middle passage" from Africa to the West Indies, usually Barbados. Many slaves died from malnutrition and disease during this voyage. When the ship reached the West Indies, the slaves were sold, and molasses and sugar were purchased. The ship then returned to Newport, and the cycle began all over again.

Many farmers in Rhode Island owned slaves, who worked the fields. Some people in Newport kept slaves as house servants, too. In 1774, due to the Quaker influence in its government, Rhode Island passed a law stopping the importation of slaves. In 1784, another law was passed that freed any slave born after March 1 of that year, once the child reached a certain age (18 for girls, 21 for boys). In 1787, Rhode Islanders were prohibited from participating in the slave trade at all, though not from owning slaves. The laws were the first of their kind passed in the former British colonies.

LIFE ON THE PLANTATIONS

Most of the land in the old Narragansett Country was divided up into large farms called plantations. A family who owned land used it to grow many crops, including corn, oats, potatoes, turnips, onions, and beans. Usually the owners had help, either hired servants or slaves.

Women on the plantation grew garden vegetables for the family's meals and cooked in large iron pots over an open flame. Women might be seamstresses or quilters. Besides housework, women also scoured the fields for herbs, barks, and roots, which could be dried and used to make medicines.

apprentice—one bound by legal agreement to work for another for a specific amount of time in return for instruction in a trade

Young people worked for their families until they were old enough to become apprentices and learn a trade. An apprentice lived with his master's family and had to serve him faithfully. In return, the master taught the apprentice his trade and how to read, write, and do simple math.

PROVIDENCE

Over the years, Providence shifted from a farming town to a merchant port. Up until about 1740, the town had not changed much from its earliest days. Houses were still laid out in a row along the main street, with farmland extending behind. A few warehouses and wharves were being built before 1700, and in 1711, a shipmaker named Nathaniel Brown began to work there. The shipbuilding industry grew, spurring Providence's growth into a seaport. The main goods that were traded out of the town were lumber and horses, but after 1740, privateering helped the port town grow. Some slavers also sailed out of Providence.

MOSES BROWN

As a child, Moses Brown spent time on the wharves in Providence. As molasses barrels were loaded, they sometimes dripped a little bit, and Moses was there to catch the drippings and taste them. When a buyer asked an importer which cask of molasses was best, the importer replied, *"Ask that little molasses-faced Moses; he will tell you."* Moses became so good at judging molasses that he went into the business with his older brother. His brother's business, Nicholas Brown and Company, took part in the West Indies molasses trade and also manufactured candles.

As he got older, Moses became interested in textile manufacturing. He formed a new company with the idea of building a cotton mill in Rhode Island. With the help of Samuel Slater, the company constructed the first water-driven cotton mill in America. It was known as Slater Mill and was located in Pawtucket, just north of Providence. Later in life, Moses became a champion of education. In 1804, the College of Rhode Island was renamed Brown University in recognition of a gift from Moses and Nicholas Brown.

In 1764, Rhode Island College was founded in Providence (it later became Brown University). True to the Rhode Island spirit, no exams were ever given about religious ideas. While "religious controversies" could be discussed, no particular Protestant sect's beliefs were taught.

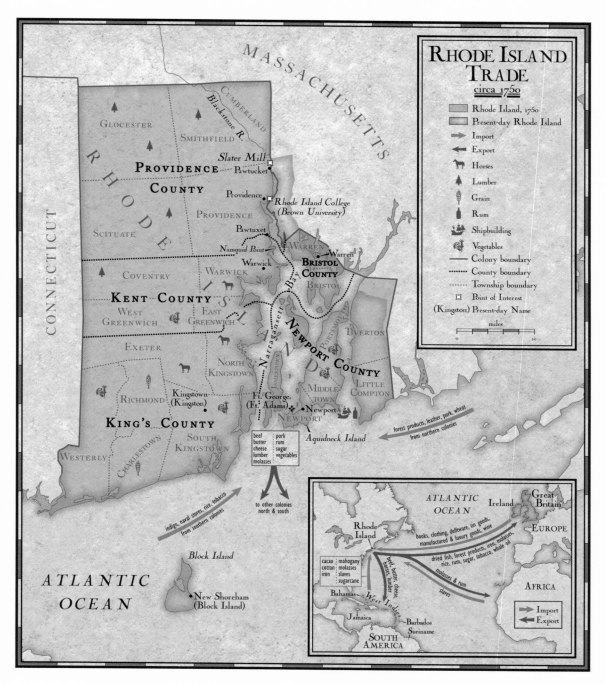

RHODE ISLAND TRADE
circa 1750

Rhode Island, 1750
Present-day Rhode Island
Import
Export
Horses
Lumber
Grain
Rum
Shipbuilding
Vegetables
Colony boundary
County boundary
Township boundary
Point of Interest
(Kingston) Present-day Name
miles
0   10

MASSACHUSETTS

CONNECTICUT

RHODE ISLAND

GLOCESTER
SMITHFIELD
CUMBERLAND
Blackstone R.

PROVIDENCE COUNTY
Slater Mill
Pawtucket
Providence
Rhode Island College
(Brown University)
PROVIDENCE
Pawtuxet
Namquid Point
Warwick
WARWICK
WARREN
Warren
BRISTOL COUNTY
BRISTOL

SCITUATE

COVENTRY

KENT COUNTY
WEST GREENWICH
EAST GREENWICH

Narragansett Bay
Newport County

EXETER

NORTH KINGSTOWN

PORTSMOUTH
TIVERTON

RICHMOND
Kingstown (Kingston)

Ft. George (Ft. Adams)
MIDDLETOWN
Newport
NEWPORT
LITTLE COMPTON

KING'S COUNTY
SOUTH KINGSTOWN

WESTERLY
CHARLESTOWN

Aquidneck Island

beef | pork
butter | rum
cheese | sugar
lumber | vegetables
molasses

to other colonies north & south

forest products, leather, pork, wheat from northern colonies

indigo, naval stores, rice, tobacco from southern colonies

Block Island

ATLANTIC OCEAN

New Shoreham (Block Island)

Inset map:
ATLANTIC OCEAN
Rhode Island
Ireland
Great Britain
EUROPE

books, clothing, delftware, tin goods, manufactured & luxury goods, wine

dried fish, forest products, iron, molasses, rice, rum, sugar, tobacco, whale oil

molasses & rum

slaves

cacao | mahogany
cotton | molasses
iron | slaves
| sugarcane

beef, butter, cheese, horses, lumber

AFRICA

Bahamas
West Indies
Jamaica
Barbados
Suriname
SOUTH AMERICA

Import
Export

By 1750, Rhode Island had become a major trade center. Much of the colony's commercial success was due to its ability to add value to imported raw materials and turn the new products into exports. For example, cacao, sugarcane, and molasses from the Caribbean region were made into chocolate, sugar, and rum. Much wealth was also gained from exporting slaves imported from Africa.

CHAPTER SEVEN

Revolution Calling

RHODE ISLAND'S FORTUNES *dwindle as settlers boycott British goods in response to taxes. The Daughters of Liberty form to support the fight for independence. Newport becomes a Loyalist stronghold.*

 n 1764, the British Parliament began to pass laws that imposed new taxes on the American colonies. Britain needed to recover some of the cost of its recent wars, specifically the French and Indian War in North America. The first law was the Sugar Act, which put a tax on all molasses and sugar imported into the

OPPOSITE: The fight for independence and freedom from Britain's tyranny is captured in this engraving called "Liberty in the Form of the Goddess of Youth: Giving Support to the Bald Eagle, 1796," by American artist Edward Savage. The young woman feeding an eagle, the symbol of the newly proclaimed United States of America, represents support for independence.

Colonies. Because so much of Rhode Island's economy depended on sugar and molasses, its colonists were very upset. The new taxes were seen as interfering with Rhode Island's economy.

Two British ships, the *St. John* and the *Squirrel*, were stationed in Newport Harbor to enforce the tax and to prevent smugglers from bringing sugar and molasses into the colony illegally. In July 1764, violence broke out when some colonists who protested the British tax fired cannon at the *St. John*. The next year, a rowboat from another British ship called the *Maidstone* was captured by an angry mob as it tried to land. The boat was dragged through the streets, so fast that it left a trail of sparks and was torched on the Common, or town square, by a mob.

The colonists' protests caused Parliament to repeal the Sugar Act in 1766. Parliament, however, would not back down. It followed up the Sugar Act with the passage of the Stamp Act. The Stamp Act required all colonists to purchase a royal stamp that would appear on all newspapers, business papers, and legal documents (such as wills, deeds to property, and licenses). There was also a tax on the paper that bore the royal stamp.

repeal—to revoke or take away, especially by an official or formal act

Like colonists elsewhere, Rhode Islanders believed that these acts infringed on their rights. The colony's government was supposed to be the only legislative body able to tax Rhode Islanders. Governor Hopkins wrote in complaint to King George III, "We have hitherto possessed . . . equal freedom with your majesty's subjects in Britain, whose essential privilege it is to be governed only by laws to which [they] themselves have some way consented, and not to be compelled to part with their property [except] . . . by authority of such laws." The treatment the colonists had received, Hopkins said, put them "in the miserable condition of slaves."

A 19th-century colored engraving shows young boys from Patriot families making fun of a Tory, or Loyalist.

The Stamp Act went into effect on November 1, 1765. Rhode Islanders ignored it, going about business as usual and refusing to use the stamps. The colony official put in charge of carrying out the new tax was Augustus Johnston, a Rhode Islander appointed by the British government. He was soon forced to resign the position. When British officials asked for the stamped papers, Johnston replied, "I am [afraid] that if any attempt should be made by me to . . . execute [the] office, without the consent of the inhabitants of the colony, that my life and property would be endangered."

In response to the Stamp Act, Rhode Island and Britain's other American colonies began boycotting British goods. Under pressure from British merchants who were losing business, Parliament repealed the Stamp Act in February 1766. In Providence, there was a great celebration. The *Providence Gazette* newspaper wrote, "*Joy and gladness shone in every countenance[face]; and nothing was to be heard but mutual congratulations. . . . [The people] marched . . . , with drums beating, trumpets sounding, and colors [flags] displayed.*"

boycott—to refuse to purchase goods from a nation or company

In 1767, Parliament passed the Townshend Acts, creating more taxes on items such as tea, glass, lead, and paper. Under the Quartering Act, British soldiers sent to America were to be fed by the colonists and given room to sleep in their houses. Once again, the colonists boycotted the taxed goods. Over the next five years, Rhode Island became very poor because many of those goods were important to the colony's economy. The state of affairs in the Colonies was summed up by one of the Providence Sons of

Daughters of LIBERTY

IN MOST COLONIES, ORGANIZATIONS called the Sons of Liberty were created in response to the Stamp Act. They planned demonstrations to protest the law and organized the boycotts of British goods. In Rhode Island, there was also a group for women called the Daughters of Liberty. It began in Providence, but by the eve of the Revolution, the Daughters had spread throughout the colony.

The Daughters of Liberty resolved to help in the fight for liberty any way they could. *"We do not mean to take up arms, for that does not become our sex: But we will put our hands to the plough, hoe and rake, and till the ground, for our men to go to the assistance of our distressed brethren. . . . We will forsake the gaieties of this world, content ourselves to live in solentary [solitary] caves, on bread and water, before we will give up our country's liberties and religion."*

Liberty, who thought that Britain had imposed the Quartering Act only to scare the colonists into obeying the tax laws: *"A standing army in time of profound peace is . . . quartered about the country to awe and intimidate the people. [Armed ships] are in every port, to the great distress of trade."* He also felt that it was time for colonists to act: *"Unless we exert ourselves . . . sentry boxes will be set up in all streets and passages, and none of us will be able to pass without being [stopped] by a soldier with his fixed bayonet, and giving him a satisfactory account of ourselves and business. . . . We will be free men or we will die."*

THE BURNING OF THE *GASPEE*

In March 1772, the British ship *Gaspee* arrived in Narragansett Bay, commanded by Lieutenant William Dudingston, with orders to enforce the acts of trade by stopping smugglers. The ship began harassing every vessel it came across in the bay. *"She suffers no vessel to pass...without a strict examination; and where any sort of unwillingness is discovered, they are compelled to submit by an armed force,"* wrote the deputy governor. The Rhode Island sailors, however, soon learned how to avoid the *Gaspee* by using decoys. One fast ship would attract the *Gaspee's* attention and lure it into a chase. Meanwhile, other ships were able to enter the port without being harassed.

By June, the colonists had had enough. On June 9, 1772, the *Gaspee* pursued a ship named the *Hannah*, which was returning home to Providence from New York. The *Hannah* led the *Gaspee* into shallow waters near Warwick. The *Gaspee* ran aground on a sandbar near Namquid Point, just as the tide was going out. The ship was stuck until the tide came back, which would not be until after midnight.

Staying out of range of the *Gaspee's* cannon, the *Hannah* sailed to Providence, where the captain reported what had happened to the ship's owner, John Brown. Realizing that the *Gaspee* would not be free for hours, Brown hatched a plan to attack the grounded ship. He gathered men, longboats, and weapons, and in the middle of the night, eight boats moved silently toward the *Gaspee*.

longboat—the longest boat carried by a sailing ship

One of the Rhode Islanders, Ephraim Bowen, recalled what happened then:

[we] proceeded until about 60 yards of the Gaspee, when a sentinel hailed, "Who comes there?" No answer. He hailed again, and no answer. In about a minute Dudingston mounted the starboard gunwale in his shirt and hailed, "Who comes there?" No answer. . . . As soon as Dudingston began to hail, Joseph Bucklin, who was standing . . . by my right side, said to me, "Eph, reach me your gun, I can kill that fellow." I reached it to him accordingly, when during Captain Whipple's replying, Bucklin fired and Dudingston fell and Bucklin exclaimed, "I have killed the rascal."

The British ship *Gaspee* burns in Narragansett Bay on June 9, 1772, as Rhode Islanders and their British prisoners watch from boats nearby.

The colonists boarded the *Gaspee* and the British sailors were tied up and then taken ashore. Lieutenant Dudington's wound was treated by a doctor with the boarding party. The *Gaspee* was then set on fire and burned right down to the water.

The British, of course, were furious. Huge rewards were offered for information about the attack, but no one claimed the money.

In 1774, the Rhode Island General Assembly proposed that the Colonies unite. It resolved, *"that a firm and inviolable union of all the colonies, in councils and measures, is absolutely necessary for the [protection] of their rights and liberties."*

Rhode Island began preparing its militia for war. Cannon were removed from Fort George, on an island near Newport, to keep them from being seized by the British. Muskets, bullets, and gunpowder were stockpiled, and the militia was ordered to *"march to the assistance of any of our sister colonies when invaded or attacked."* In April 1775, the first shots of the American Revolution were fired in Massachusetts. After the battle at Lexington, the Rhode Island government called for 1,500 more men to join the militia.

The winter of 1775 brought hard times for Rhode Island. Another British ship, the *Rose*, which had about ten other armed ships under her command, was harassing Newport. The ships stopped molasses trade, disrupted the mail (which was delivered by ferry), and threatened to destroy Newport if the sailors aboard were not given livestock for food. The people of Newport suffered. *"The vast number of poor . . . that are destitute of almost every necessary of life . . . cannot subsist long."* Many people left the city, seeking refuge on the mainland. A truce was made with the *Rose* eventually, but the movement toward war continued through the winter and spring of 1776.

A colonial woman holding a musket takes up the cause for independence as her husband, a minuteman in the colonial militia, leaves for battle during the American Revolution.

LOYALISTS

Not every colonist favored independence from Britain. Some were still loyal to the British crown, although they were certainly the minority in Rhode Island. Loyalists were most numerous in Newport. The wealthy people there wanted Rhode Island to remain a British colony because they had become rich under that system. Loyalists were not popular. The colony even passed laws to punish them, which had the effect of driving most of them away.

The governor elected in 1775, just before the battles of Lexington and Concord in Massachusetts, was Joseph Wanton. Wanton was a Loyalist who believed that the best way to keep Rhode Island's charter freedoms safe was by staying loyal to the King. When the General Assembly voted to enlist 1,500 men in the militia, Governor Wanton refused to sign the orders for the militia officers to command the new recruits, saying it would be *subversive of the true interest of this government.* The General Assembly then stripped Wanton of power, and in November 1775 appointed a new governor—Nicholas Cooke. Cooke, who had been deputy governor, was a supporter of independence from Britain.

On May 4, 1776, the Rhode Island Assembly voted to sever its ties with the King and Great Britain. Rhode Island's act came a full two months earlier than the Declaration of

Independence by Congress, making Rhode Island the first colony to declare its independence from Britain:

> WHEREAS, George the Third, King of Great Britain, . . . entirely departing from the duties and character of a good King, instead of protecting, is endeavoring to destroy the good people of this Colony, and of all the United Colonies, by sending fleets and armies to America to confiscate our property, and spread fire, sword and desolation throughout our country, in order to compel us to submit to the most debasing and detestable tyranny; whereby it becomes our highest duty, to use every means with which God and nature have furnished us, in support of our inviolable rights and privileges, to oppose that power which is exerted only for our destruction. �֎

CHAPTER EIGHT

Revolution and Union

THE BRITISH OCCUPY NEWPORT *during the Revolutionary War. Rhode Island becomes the first state to ratify the Articles of Confederation, but it is the last of the 13 Colonies to ratify the Constitution.*

lthough no major battles of the Revolution happened in Rhode Island, the colony did raise troops to aid the Continental Army, which was the military force commanded by General George Washington. The army was organized by the Continental Congress, a body of representatives from each of the colonies that met in Philadelphia as a united government for the Colonies. A regiment of "*negro, mulatto,*

OPPOSITE: A colonel (atop horse) and private of the First Continental Rhode Island Infantry patrol a Rhode Island town.

and Indian slaves" was created and later merged with the rest of Rhode Island's division. As a dedicated seafaring colony, Rhode Island became responsible for the creation of the American Navy, as well.

A portrait of Esek Hopkins, first commodore of the U.S. Navy

In 1775, the Rhode Island delegates to the Continental Congress proposed *"the building and equipping at the continental expense of an American fleet."* By February 1776, a fleet of six ships was built. The navy was put under the command of

Rhode Islander Esek Hopkins. Unfortunately, this navy was not much of a success. It did not seriously damage a single British ship that it encountered, and Hopkins had trouble recruiting sailors. Privateers were also being commissioned to attack British ships, and sailors flocked to those ships, where they could make much more money.

BRITISH OCCUPATION

In December 1776, British forces appeared off the coast of Block Island. On December 9, 6,000 British troops landed on Rhode Island, marched into Newport, and took over the city. The enemy's overwhelming numbers had caused the city's small defense force of only a few hundred men to retreat to the mainland before the British arrived. And so began the British occupation of Newport. It lasted three years.

At first, General Washington thought the British were preparing to attack Providence and the rest of New England, but as the winter progressed and the troops made no moves, it became clear that the British were simply finding winter quarters. General Washington was content to let the British troops remain inactive in Newport. Those 6,000 troops in Rhode Island meant 6,000 fewer troops in New York and New Jersey, where the real fighting had been taking place.

The British occupiers took over the town. A Newport resident and Patriot named Fleet S. Green kept a diary that

Patriot—a colonist who favored independence from Britain

describes the bad treatment of the residents by the British soldiers, who were called "red-backs" or "lobster-backs" because of the red coats they traditionally wore:

> *July 15, 1777. The sole command of the town is invested in Major Barry. . . . He abuses the inhabitant, friends of Liberty in the most shocking manner, not [allowing] them to talk in the streets, struck Mr. Fairchild for not taking off his hat to a gentleman, as [Barry] styled himself.*

> *Oct. 2. This morning all the furniture and wearing apparel was seized by order of [British] General Pigot.*

> *Oct. 22. This morning 73 of the principle inhabitants were sent on board the prison ship under Hessian [German soldiers serving with the British Army for pay] guards followed by great numbers of women and children, who were not suffered to speak to their husbands and parents.*

> *Oct. 23. The soldiers and sailors continue to steal potatoes, corn, and other [food] from the inhabitants.*

The French fleet, commanded by Comte d'Estaing, approaches Newport on August 8, 1778, in anticipation of engaging Britain's Navy in battle.

In February 1778, France allied itself with the Americans against its old enemy, Great Britain. In August 1778, the American forces devised a plan to attack the British near Newport, with help from their new French allies. The American troops would attack the fort by land from one side, while the French Navy and Marines attacked from the sea on the other. But as they prepared for the attack, a strong hurricane arose, and the French fleet was forced to sail to Boston for repairs. The French fleet never returned, and the American forces that had landed on Rhode Island had to retreat because there was no hope of victory. The British tried to overrun them, but the Americans were able to beat the British back long enough to escape to the mainland. This event has become known as the Battle of Rhode Island.

A Loyalist's DIARY

MARY GOULD ALMY OF Newport was a staunch Tory. Her husband, Benjamin Almy, a soldier in Rhode Island's militia, believed strongly in the cause of freedom. Despite their difference of political opinion, Mary Almy remained a loving wife who constantly worried about her husband's safety. She kept a diary that was written as a letter to her husband: *"Tuesday, August 18 [1778]. Awake early, the night one continual dreading, you ever the subject; sometimes you were before me all pleasantness, your countenance like yourself when happy; then again, all was distress; fighting, firing and every horror that my fear forebode, when awake. Oh! That it was at an end! That I knew the worst!"*

A DARING RAID

In July 1777, a Continental Army general named Charles Lee was captured by the British. General Lee would not be returned until the Americans had captured a British general to use as an exchange. On July 10, 1777, a group of Rhode Island men did just that.

William Barton was from the town of Warren, Rhode Island, and a lieutenant colonel in the militia. He learned that a British general, Richard Prescott, often stayed with a Loyalist named Overing, outside the British fortifications. Just before midnight, Barton and 40 men in five boats slipped past the British ships. They overpowered the soldier on sentry duty, burst into Overing's house, and seized General Prescott.

Captain Frederick Mackenzie, an officer of the British force in Newport, wrote of the raid in his diary:

The Rebels certainly run a great risk in making this attempt; as a shot fired by the Sentry would have given the alarm. . . . They however executed it in a masterly manner, and deserve credit for the attempt. It is certainly a most extraordinary circumstance, that a General commanding a body of 4000 men, encamped on an island surrounded by a squadron of ships of war, should be carried off from his quarters in the night by a small party of the enemy from without, and without a shot being fired.

The British left Newport in October 1779. The city had lost all its former glory and prosperity. Newport, and Rhode Island as a whole, had become so poor that the governor had been asking the other states for help over the last two years. Thankfully, the states were united in the cause of independence, and Rhode Island got the aid it needed.

RHODE ISLAND JOINS THE UNION

While the Revolutionary War raged, the business of government had to be taken care of. In order to create a union of the states, the Continental Congress submitted the Articles of Confederation to the states for approval in November 1777. The idea was thought to be *"essential to our very existence as a free people."* The Articles created a weak federal government. With the memory of British tyranny fresh in their minds, the states did not want a strong central government. Under the Articles, representatives of the states met in Congress, which could make decisions about national concerns but was powerless to enforce them.

In February 1778, Rhode Island became the first of the newly declared states to ratify the Articles of Confederation. The weak federal government was just what Rhode Island wanted. Under the Articles, each state kept its *"sovereignty, freedom, and independence,"* so Rhode Islanders knew that they would continue to enjoy their religious and civil freedoms. Congress could not make laws affecting a state's trade and had no power to tax the states. The Articles could be changed only if every state agreed.

In 1781, as the Revolutionary War came to an end with the British surrender at Yorktown, Congress declared that it was necessary to begin taxing all goods imported into the United States. A national convention was called to amend the Articles to give Congress the power to collect taxes. Rhode Island would not accept the amendment. Merchants were afraid that a tax would reduce their profits, and Rhode Island was still a poor state after years of British occupation. For five years, the state stayed firm in its stand against the tax, a decision that prevented the amendment from passing throughout the nation. But by 1786, it realized that the tax was necessary to stop a flood of British-manufactured products. Rhode Island reluctantly agreed to support the import tax.

In 1787, a new crisis occurred—the proposal of a new federal Constitution. The Articles of Confederation had failed because the federal government had no power to make the states comply with its laws. Rhode Island's resistance to the taxation issue in 1781 had demonstrated another problem with the Articles. The fact that the veto of a single state was enough to prevent changes in the Federal government meant that Congress was almost powerless to effectively govern the Union. In March 1787, Congress held a convention in Philadelphia to create a stronger federal government and thus a more powerful union.

At the time, Rhode Island's state government was under the control of farmers, who did not depend on trade with the other states for their livelihood. They did not care about federal matters as much as the merchants who relied on interstate trade. As a result, Rhode Island did not send representatives to the convention.

French artist Laurent Deroy painted this view of Providence as it looked in the 1700s. By then, it was already a thriving port city.

Because of the difficulty of changing the Articles, Congress decided to create an entirely new government. In September, it submitted the U.S. Constitution to the states for ratification. The Constitution would go into effect once nine states had accepted it. Rhode Islanders, especially the farmers, were afraid that the proposed federal government, with its many new powers, would be able to take away their freedoms. In 1788, a writer for the *Newport Mercury* newspaper wrote, *"If you adopt the proposed Constitution, you will subject yourselves to a government where you will be totally unprotected by a bill of rights."*

In 1788 and 1789, the Rhode Island General Assembly refused seven times to call a constitutional convention for the purpose of ratifying the Constitution. But the United States forced the issue in July 1789, when Congress passed a tax on all foreign imports. The law made no exception for Rhode Island, and merchants, concentrated in the busy port of Providence, were upset. The import tax would drastically affect the profits they derived from importing foreign goods and reselling them throughout the U.S. The United States had dropped hints that if Rhode Island did not join the rest of the states, it would be treated as a foreign nation. Providence threatened to secede from the rest of Rhode Island and join the Union on its own.

Finally, in March 1790, Rhode Island called a convention. Around the same time, the first ten amendments, known as the Bill of Rights, were added to the Constitution. The Bill of Rights eased many people's fears by guaranteeing many freedoms for American citizens, such as freedom of speech and religion. It also limited the power of the federal government because it gave the states all the powers that were not specifically given to

Congress. At the convention on May 29, 1790 Rhode Island voted to ratify the Constitution by a vote of 34 to 32. By accepting the Constitution as the "law of the land," Rhode Island became the last of the original thirteen colonies to join the United States.

Rhode Island's history is ultimately a story of hope. The first settlers hoped for a place where they would be free to worship according to their own consciences. The men and women who fought to gain and keep the broad freedoms of Rhode Island's charter did so to ensure that those freedoms would continue indefinitely. And the Patriots who struggled in the Revolution to win independence for the United States continued those strong hopes. It seems fitting, therefore, that ever since 1666 Rhode Island's state motto has been *"Hope."*

The present-day seal of the State of Rhode Island, which features an anchor beneath the motto "Hope," is the same image used on the seal of the Providence Plantations (shown here) in the mid 1600s.

TIME LINE

1524 Giovanni da Verrazano is the first European explorer to visit the Narragansett Bay area.

1614 Adrian Block visits an island in Narragansett Bay and names it for himself.

1634 William Blackstone begins living at Study Hill, near the Pawtucket River in what becomes Cumberland, Rhode Island.

1636 Banished from Massachusetts Bay Colony for his religious ideas, Roger Williams settles land given to him by the Narragansett sachems.

1638 Another group of outcasts from Massachusetts Bay, including Anne and William Hutchinson, John Clarke, and William Coddington, found Pocasset, later renamed Portsmouth.

1639 Coddington and Clarke leave Pocasset to found Newport.

1643 Samuel Gorton and his followers settle at Shawomet, later renamed Warwick.

1644 Roger Williams obtains a charter from Parliament, which is the first official British recognition of the colony.

1649 Claiming he discovered and purchased the area, William Coddington obtains a royal charter naming him governor for life of Aquidneck Island, where Portsmouth and Newport are located.

1651 Roger Williams and John Clarke travel to England and get Coddington's charter revoked.

1657 The first Quakers arrive in Newport aboard the *Woodhouse*.

1663 John Clarke obtains a royal charter for the colony. It remains Rhode Island's basic law until 1843.

1675 Rapidly declining relations between the United Colonies of New England and Native Americans lead to King Philip's War, which nearly wipes out the Indian population.

1676 More than 50 houses in Providence are burned down in the last months of King Philip's War.

1686 French Huguenots settle East Greenwich.

1711 Shipbuilder Nathaniel Brown begins working in Providence, and the town soon becomes a busy port.

1764 The British Parliament orders strict enforcement of the Sugar Act, the first in a series of taxes that angers Rhode Islanders. Colonists protest in Newport.

1767 Parliament passes the Townshend Acts, which include a law forcing the colonists to house and feed British troops.

1772 Rhode Islanders burn the *Gaspee* in the first American act of violence against the British.

1774 The Rhode Island General Assembly proposes that the Colonies unite to protect their civil liberties.

1776 In May, Rhode Island becomes the first colony to declare its independence from Britain. In December, British troops begin a three-year occupation of Newport.

1778 Rhode Island ratifies the Articles of Confederation.

1779 The British occupation of Newport ends.

1781 The British surrender at Yorktown, effectively ending the American Revolution.

1787 The Constitutional Convention is called in Philadelphia to create a strong federal government. Rhode Island does not send delegates.

1790 Under threats that it would be treated as a foreign nation by the United States, Rhode Island finally joins the Union, the last of the original 13 British colonies to do so.

RESOURCES

BOOKS

Doherty, Craig A. and Katherine M. *Rhode Island (Thirteen Colonies)*. New York: Facts on File, 2005.

Fradin, Dennis B. *The Rhode Island Colony (Thirteen Colonies)*. Connecticut: Children's Press, 1989.

Gray, Edward G. *Colonial America, A History in Document*. New York, NY: Oxford University Press, 2003.

McLoughlin, William. *Rhode Island, A History (States and the Nation)*. New York: W.W. Norton & Company, 1986.

Middleton, Richard. *Colonial America: A History 1565–1776*. Malden, MA: Blackwell Publishing, 2000.

WEB SITES

Know Rhode Island
http://www.sec.state.ri.us/library/riinfo/riinfo/knowrhode The Rhode Island Secretary of State Web site contains a brief overview of Rhode Island's history, important people, and fun facts about the state.

Hall of North and South Americans
http://www.famousamericans.net/
Contains short biographies of many important figures in Rhode Island's history.

Gaspee Virtual Archives
http://www.gaspee.org/
site dedicated to the burning of the *Gaspee*.

http://www.dickshovel.com/up.html
History of about 240 Native American tribes, including those important to Rhode Island.

http://americaslibrary.gov/cgi-bin/page.cgi
The Library of Congress's Web site for kids contains information about Rhode Island and other American colonies.

http://www.slavenorth.com/rhodeisland.htm
This site details the practice of slavery in Rhode Island and the other northern colonies.

QUOTE SOURCES

CHAPTER ONE

pp. 14–15 "we discovered...along the coast." Lippincott, Bertram. *Indians, Privateers, and High Society.* Philadelphia and New York: J.B. Lippincott Company, 1961, p. 21; p. 15 "[God] knows...doubting conscience." Easton, Emily. *Roger Williams: Prophet and Pioneer.* New York: AMS Press, 1970, p. 133; p. 17 "God sent you...not a Playhouse." Taylor, Alan. *American Colonies: The Settling of North America.* New York: Penguin, Reprint edition 2002, p. 162; p. 18 "I spake on...for my bread." Carpenter, Edmund J. *Roger Williams: A Study of the Life, Times, and Character of a Political Pioneer.* New York: The Grafton Press, 1909, p. 42; p. 19 "Mr. Roger Williams...some thing abruptly." Bicknell, Thomas Williams. *Story of Dr. John Clarke.* Published by the author, 1915, Volume 1, p. 125; pp. 19–20 "disputed...with the natives." Carpenter, pp. 44–45; p. 20 "Whereas Mr. Roger...from the Court." Carpenter, p. 103; p. 22 "I was...bed did mean." Easton, p. 177; p. 23 "Since I was...as themselves." Carpenter, p. 127.

CHAPTER TWO

p. 29 "How could ye...OUR KING!" www.pequotwar.com; pp. 30–31 "God was...gain their tongue." Lippincott, Bertram, *Indians, Privateers, and High Society.* Philadelphia and New York: J.B. Lippincott Company, 1961, p. 32; p. 31 "Three days and...against the Pequots." Carpenter, Edmund J. *Roger Williams: A Study of the Life, Times, and Character of a Political Pioneer.* New York: The Grafton Press, 1909, p. 151; p. 33 "I never...but by gift." Carpenter, p. 139; p. 34 "I left England...Lord Brethren." Lippincott, p. 28.

CHAPTER THREE

p. 38 "I'll bring...kind of spirit." www.harvard-magazine.com/on-line/1102194.html; p. 39 "As I understand...the pathway." www.harvard-magazine.com/on-line/1102194.html; p. 39 "In the name...of the congregation." Carroll, Charles. *Rhode Island: 3 Centuries of Democracy.* New York: Lewis Historical Publishing Company, Inc., 1932, Vol. I, p. 25; p. 41 "So to a...now Rhode Island." Carroll, Vol. I, p. 26; "It was not...Pequot War." Easton, Emily. *Roger Williams: Prophet and Pioneer.* New York: AMS Press, 1970,

pp. 209–210; p. 42 "to sell...may be useful." Lippincott, Bertram, *Indians, Privateers, and High Society.* Philadelphia and New York: J.B. Lippincott Company, 1961, p. 64.

CHAPTER FOUR

p. 48 "to enjoy liberty...other end." Lippincott, Bertram, *Indians, Privateers, and High Society.* Philadelphia and New York: J.B. Lippincott Company, 1961, p. 52; p. 49 "Master Gorton...this country." Carroll, Charles. *Rhode Island: 3 Centuries of Democracy.* New York: Lewis Historical Publishing Company, Inc., 1932, Vol. I, p. 29; "the commander...such transgressors." Carroll, p. 49; p. 50 "If you...speedily kindled." http://www.famousamericans.net/samuelgorton; "as men...slaughter." Carroll, p. 55; p. 51 "at random...unto us." http://www.famousamericans.net/samuelgorton; p. 53 "full power...place will allow." Carroll, p. 79; p. 54 "as a private...among the Barbarians." Lippincott, p. 39; p. 56 "have it much...religious concernments." Carroll, p. 96; "no person...religious concernment." Carroll, p. 97; p. 57 "with much...all the people." Carroll, p. 99.

CHAPTER FIVE

p. 61 "they delight...patient sufferings." Carroll, Charles. *Rhode Island: 3 Centuries of Democracy.* New York: Lewis Historical Publishing Company, Inc., 1932, Vol. I, p. 53; p. 62 "with wicked hands... wicked is cruelty." Lippincott, Bertram, *Indians, Privateers, and High Society.* Philadelphia and New York: J.B. Lippincott Company, 1961, p. 75; "in obedience...to the death." Lippincott, p. 75; p. 64 "dangerous pests...among you." Lippincott, p. 72; "we have no...an eternal condition." Carroll, p. 53; p. 65 "I am...no country." Lippincott, p. 80; "Not a Wampanoag...delivered up." Lippincott, p. 80; p. 67 "We marched...till night." Lippincott, pp. 83–84; "women and children...account of." Lippincott, pp. 83–84; p. 68 "you are a...shall be touched." Lippincott, p. 82; p. 69 "[I like]...of [myself]." Lippincott, p. 82.

CHAPTER SIX

p. 73 "All the vessels...kill them." Richman, Irving Berdine. *Rhode Island: A Study in Separatism.* New York & Boston: Houghton, Mifflin, &Co., 1905, p. 87;

p. 74 "Steering for...and yielded." Richman, p. 87; p. 75 "the most...King's Dominions." Richman, p. 94; "I am well...their spoils." Richman, p. 93; p. 78 "Ask that...will tell you." Richman, p. 162.

CHAPTER SEVEN

p. 83 "We have hitherto...condition of slaves." Carroll, Charles. *Rhode Island: 3 Centuries of Democracy.* New York: Lewis Historical Publishing Company, Inc., 1932, Vol. I, p. 235; p. 84 "I am [afraid]...would be endangered." Carroll, p. 244; "Joy and [flags] displayed." Carroll, p. 244; p. 85 "We do not...and religion." Lippincott, Bertram, *Indians, Privateers, and High Society.* Philadelphia and New York: J.B. Lippincott Company, 1961, p. 140; "A standing army...of trade." Carroll, p. 250; "Unless we...we will die." Carroll, p. 250; p. 86 "She suffers...armed force." Carroll, p. 252; p. 87 "[we] proceeded...the rascal." http://gaspee.org/Bowen.html; p. 88 "that a firm... and liberties." Carroll, p. 262; "march to...or attacked." http://constitution.org/jw/acm_2-m.txt; p. 89 "The vast...subsist long." Lovejoy, David S. *Rhode Island Politics and the American Revolution.* Providence: Brown University Press, 1958, p. 186; p. 90 "subversive... government." Lovejoy, p. 183; p. 91 "WHEREAS, George...for our destruction." Carroll, p. 269.

CHAPTER EIGHT

p. 94 "the building...fleet." Richman, Irving Berdine. *Rhode Island: A Study in Separatism.* New York & Boston: Houghton, Mifflin, & Co., 1905, p. 213; p. 96 "July 15, 1777...from the inhabitants." Lippincott, Bertram, *Indians, Privateers, and High Society.* Philadelphia and New York: J.B. Lippincott Company, 1961, pp. 183–184; p. 97 "Tuesday, August...knew the worst!" Lippincott, p. 173; p. 98 "The Rebels...of the enemy." Lippincott, p. 179; p. 99 "essential...free people." Carroll, Charles. *Rhode Island: 3 Centuries of Democracy.* New York: Lewis Historical Publishing Company, Inc., 1932, Vol. I, p. 353 "sovereignty, freedom, and independence." http://vagenweb.org/hening/vol01-02.htm; p. 102 "If you...bill of rights." Richman, pp. 252–253.

INDEX

ABOUT THE AUTHOR AND CONSULTANT

JESSE McDERMOTT has written a multitude of nonfiction and fiction books for middle-grade readers on topics ranging from ancient civilizations to the history of blues music. He is a graduate of Boston College and Boston University School of Law. He currently lives in Brighton, Massachusetts.

BRENDAN McCONVILLE is a professor in the Department of History at Boston University where he teaches courses on colonial America, the American Revolution, and American Politics. He received his Ph.D. from Brown University. McConville has written numerous books and articles on the early years of the American colonies. He lives in Brookline, Massachusetts.

ILLUSTRATION CREDITS

1685

NEW NORTH
WALES

NEW SOUTH
WAL

ARCT

BA
B

Chucaskaby or
Nation of Strong Men

Nadoussis

Hanetons

Heati

Menomibufini
Eltibitoni

Tinthopha
or Nation
of the Master

AGinipinale

The Gulf or
Lake of Stinking

Nadoues

LAKE SUPERIOR

Lake of Hares

L. PISCOU

LAKE
HURONS

Tract of Land
full of Wild Bulls

ILINOIS

ILLEZE

NEW NORTH

S Pedro

C.Blanco

C France
C S Sebastian
C Mendocino
C D Orleans

NEW

ALBION

SEA OF CALIFORNIA

Key Coronado

NEW

NEW MEXICO

MEXICO

MAR

MEXICO

THE GOLF OR
BAY OF
MEXICO

NEW BISCAIA

ZACATECAS

C Blanco
Coast Pescadores

MEXICO

PANUCO

S Bartholomew

S Thome

S Lazarus

S Pedro

S Bartholomew

St Peters I.

SEA

OF

NEW SPAIN

HONDRA